Common Sense DISCIPLINE

Dr. Roger Allen & Ron Rose

Christian
Parenting
BOOKS

Unless otherwise noted, Scripture quotations are from the *Holy Bible: New International Version* © 1973, 1978, 1984 by International Bible Society. Used by permission of Zondervan Bible Publishers.

Notice: This publication is designed to provide accurate and authoritative information in regard to the subject matter covered. It is sold with the understanding that the publisher is not engaged in rendering psychological, medical, or other professional services. If expert assistance or counseling is needed, the services of a competent professional should be sought.

Christian Parenting Books is an imprint of
Chariot Family Publishing, a division of
David C. Cook Publishing Co., Elgin, Illinois 60120
David C. Cook Publishing Co., Weston, Ontario
Nova Distribution Ltd., Newton Abbot, England

Christian Parenting Today Magazine
P.O. Box 850, Sisters, OR 97759 (800) 238-2221

COMMON SENSE DISCIPLINE
©1993 by Roger Allen and Ron Rose

Cover design by Foster Design Associates
Interior Design by Glass House Graphics

First Printing, 1993
Printed in the United States of America
97 96 95   5 4 3 2

CIP Applied for.
ISBN 0-78140-0125-9

In honor of the love my parents gave me,
and dedicated
to the loving and lasting memory
of my father, who taught me much
by what he chose neither to say nor do
when others acted irresponsibly.

—Roger

This book is our pledge of hope
for concerned parents
who want to be more confident
and competent
in raising responsible kids.

—Ron

Acknowledgements

From my perspective, this book would not have been possible without the practical guidance of two very special people: Myron Beard, Ph.D. of San Antonio, and Melvin Klement of New Dominion School, Dillwyn, Virginia.

In Tyler, several bookstore managers initially encouraged me to publish, including Michael Burp, Paul Herman, Trudy Richardson, and Ann Sefrna. A number of media people also helped: Joan Hallmark of Station KLTV, Robert Main and Dan Gresham, Phil Hook and Gary Lesniewski of Radio KVNE. I am also indebted to Brad Spradlin; William Stanton, M.D.; Brian Walker and Gail Wise.

Kollie and Dot-Dot showered Lane with their love while Kathy and I worked late. Chris Moch was a special help.

For all of you, I am thankful.

—Roger

From a warm spot deep in my heart, I need to acknowledge those who helped me write my parts of this book:

Julie and Joy, two terrific kids who gave me ideas and insights and kept the book focused on the real world.

Lyn, my inspiring wife, who encouraged and evaluated every word and comma. I especially appreciate her tireless efforts at entering this manuscript into the word processor.

Thelma and John Rose for the gift of life and the years of love, thank you forever.

—Ron

Both of us are grateful to Byron Williamson, who in his own way encouraged us to excellence.

But most of all, for the talents which make our work possible and permit us to provide for our families while helping others, we thank God.

Roger B. Allen, Ph.D.   Ron Rose
Tyler, TX   N. Richland Hills, TX

Foreword

Ever since I wrote *Kids Say the Darndest Things*, people have been sending me funny stories about children. One of them concerns a little boy standing on his porch crying and rubbing his backside. When a kindly old gentleman asked what was the trouble, the youngster replied, "My daddy lost his psychology book, and now he's using common sense."

I am excited about this book, *Common Sense Discipline*, because it is the practical approach to parenting that is exactly what moms and dads need.

Perhaps more now than at any period in history the fiber of family life is in danger of being torn to shreds. Collapsing family life leads to sick children, who become sick adults, who create a sick nation.

If parents would follow the recommendations in this book, I believe our families would be stronger and safer. It is filled with words of wisdom, and it encourages parents to trust themselves and use common sense.

I like it.

—Art Linkletter

Introduction

RAISING CHILDREN IS A NEVER ENDING, in-process, learn-as-you-go kind of job. For many of us, it seems that when we're working hardest at it, we are criticized the most. When a child goes wrong, for instance, we parents become the "blamees" of choice. Yet, while we may have been taught Chaucer and calculus in school, we probably received little, if any, on-the-job training to prepare us for raising children. No matter how hard we work, how much overtime we put in, someone will question what we do. And frequently our worst critic is our own child.

As parents, we often get blamed for much that is wrong in our society, from the violence in the streets to lower national averages on the Scholastic Aptitude Test. However, in spite of all the pressures working to dismantle our influence, we continue to be the most important adults in the lives of our children. We still have the power. We still enjoy the opportunity to be the best coach, the wisest teacher, the most caring counselor, and the greatest hero our children will ever know.

Looking for Parenting Help?

Since 1968 we have been working with families from all walks of life, trying to help them find solutions to their parenting problems. The children have ranged from normal, ordinary kids to those with severe emotional handicaps. Some were visually impaired; others had multiple physical handicaps. Their parents ranged from Christian to atheist, well-educated to illiterate, rich to poor, liberal to conservative. The common dream of all of these parents was a driving desire to do a better job raising their children.

This book is for anyone, then, who wants to know what to do and say as a parent. In these pages you'll discover how to help your children grow into responsible adults by putting practical insights and suggestions to use on a daily basis. No one has all the answers to parenting questions, and, in fact, we are still discovering many of the most important questions to ask. However, by squarely facing the questions most frequently asked by parents, *Common Sense Discipline* helps you develop confidence in your own parenting style, likely releasing loads of pent-up fear and doubt.

If this is your first lap around the track with kids, then know that this type of training is just the beginning. Starting out right means developing the best overall game plan for each child. Wise strategies and a good amount of endurance will then carry you through.

You're Not Alone!

The Bible is full of stories of parents who faced tough times. Imagine Eve, the world's first mother, wondering in anguish, "Where did we go wrong with Cain?" Or consider Job, who, at a high point in his life, saw his whole family and fortune suddenly wiped out. Even Mary and Joseph must have had their parenting struggles. Certainly Jesus' parents provided excellent guidance and supervision, yet they didn't always understand what was going on in their young child's mind (see Luke 2:50). Just when things seemed to be looking the best for Jesus, He was killed by an ungrateful mob. Do you suppose Mary ever thought, "If only . . ."?

So you're not alone if you've found kids to be a tough course of study. If your baby was easy—never had colic, never got fussy, and started sleeping through the night at two weeks old—congratulations! You were fortunate. But if you're having trouble with your child, we know the pain you feel. If your preschool child has scared you and made you wonder what sort of adult he's going to be, we've heard your story. If your teenager is sullen, disobedient, sassy, and disrespectful, you are not alone. In short, if you're looking for some common sense help with your kids, read on!

—Roger and Ron

Contents

1 A Common Sense Starting Place **19**

Learning from Your Parents' Imperfections............................20

Surveying the Essential Skills 22

Providing Support 23

Setting Limits 24

Recognizing Your Parenting Style...25

    Boss 25

    Friend..26

    Provider 26

    Nurturer 27

Avoiding Three Common Sources of Frustration 27

Adjusting Your Personal Balance 30

2 The Basics of Common Sense Discipline **33**

Responsibility: The Common Sense Goal 34

Negative Attention: A Motive for Misbehavior 36

Values: The Character-Development Challenge 39

Family Health: What Can We Do?.......................................41

3 Showing Love and Support **43**

Modeling Values..43

Exploring New Worlds 45

Questioning and Reflecting 46

Empowering 48

Playing 50
Comforting in Failure...................................51
Hugging and Touching................................52
Demonstrating Love 52
4 Setting Limits and Controlling Behavior 55
The Triangle Perspective 56
Catch 'Em Doing Something Right 56
The Power of a Positive Word 57
    Start Right Now 58
Logical Consequences 58
    Consequences Speak Loudly 59
    Natural Consequences 59
    Schedules and Promises 60
    Fines and Penalties 60
Time-out 62
    Getting Started Right 62
    Time-out for Small Children 63
    The Place for Time-out 64
    Giving Instructions Once 65
Negative Practice 66
Punishment 67
    Spanking 67
    Spanking Older Kids 68
    Paddling 68
    Potential Problems with Punishment 69
Character Testing...70
Key to Success 71
Considering the Options 72
5 Guiding Their First Steps—12-30 Months 73
The Nature of Love 73
First Six Months 75
    Walking 76
    When Your Child Is Hurt 76
    Baby-Proofing Your House 77

Christmas Trees 78
Talking 79
Fussing 80
Toilet Training 80
If Your Child Has an Accident 81
Using a Star Chart 82
The Temporary Twos 83
Tantrums 84
Public Demonstrations 84
Where Do They Learn That? 85
Typical Childhood Fears 86
Fear of Strangers 86
Fear of Separation 86
Baby Sitters 87
How to Prepare the Baby Sitter 87
Leaving Baby Overnight 88
Now I Have Some Options 88

6 Exploring the World with Limits 91
3-5 Years..91
Conversations of Wonder 92
Parent Preparation 94
Remain Flexible 95
Traveling with Small Children.............................96
When Parents Are Gone for the Night................97
Tattling...98
Are You Ready for Pets?..98
Managing Aggression 99
Biting 99
Fussing and Fighting 99
Fistfights and Wrestling......................................100
Playing Sick 101
Relieving Fears..102
Nightmares 102
Serious Illness...103

When Someone Dies 104
Security Blankets 105
Thumb Sucking 106
Bedtime Problems 107
Nightly Routines 108
Distractions at Bedtime 108
When Parents Disagree 109
A Typical Day with Common Sense Discipline 110

7 Helping Kids Learn Self-Control 113
6-11 Years 113
The GAS Trap 113
The Guilt Trip 114
Fits of Anger 114
The Silent Treatment 115
GAS and the Stepparent 116
Three Critical Lessons 118
Reliability 118
    Resourcefulness 118
    Responsibility 118
Suzy and the Three Rs 118
Your Plan for Children with Self-Discipline 120
1. Talk It Out 121
2. Get Inside Their Heads 121
3. Make the Rules 122
4. Break It Down 123
    Assignment Chart 124
    Fun Charts 124
    Incentive Charts 125
5. Show Them How 125
6. What Will Happen 126
7. Did It Work? 128
Are Your Expectations Realistic? 129

8 Solutions That Make Sense 131
6-11 Years 131

Early Morning Tensions 132
Haggling with Homework 133
Resistance to Reading 134
Fears and Failures 135
The Fear of Trying 136
Failing in School 137
Clothes, Closets, and Cooperation 138
Ideas for Clothes Care 139
Scattered Clothes 139
TV: Adopted or Adapted 140
When Meanness Hurts 141
    Intervene 141
    Listen 143
    Tell about something similar happening to you 143
    Encourage your child to do something kind 143
Allowances and Money Matters 144
Erasing Four-Letter Words 145
Eliminating Lying 146
Bullies and Bandits 147
Breaking Bad Habits 147
Accepting Limitations 148
Reviewing Your Perspective 148
9 Common Sense with Sensitive Ears 151
11-14 Years: Do You Know These Young Teens?.............151
Ron's Story...151
Keri's Story..153
What's Behind the Face? 155
Putting the Pieces Together..157
The Nine Most Repeated Sayings 158
    "It's Not Fair!"..158
        Cheating 159
        Cleaning...160
        Moving 160
    "Why Can't I. . ." 161

... do what I want?" 161
... go where I want?" 161
... talk like I want?" 161
"How Embarrassing!" 162
　　Keri and Her Body 162
　　Kevin and His Body 162
"I Don't Have Anything to Wear!" 164
　　Fashion and Fads 164
"It Wasn't My Fault!" 164
　　Blaming Others 164
　　Coping with Failure 166
　　Fighting with Friends/Siblings 166
"I'm Not a Kid Anymore!" 167
　　Deciding about Drugs and Alcohol 167
　　Deciding about Tobacco 169
　　Deciding about Sex 169
　　Deciding about Faith 170
"You Don't Understand!" 171
　　Going Together 171
　　Breaking Up 171
　　Silence 172
　　Distrust 172
　　Almost Grown 173
　　How to Talk to Your Teen about Virginity 173

10 Put the Monkey on Their Back 175
15-18 Years 175
Who's in Charge 176
Developing Independence 177
　　Setting Goals 177
Priority or Privacy 178
The Bedroom 178
Accepting Personal Likes 180
Freedom and the Automobile 183
Trust Your Teenager as a Driver 183

Drinking and Driving 184
Making Decisions on Their Own 185
Checklist for Helping Teens Make Decisions 185
Coping with Anxiety...186
Understanding the Silent Worries................................187
Handling Conflict..188
Discuss Controversial Issues 189
Curfew Conflict 190
Critical Attitude 191
Going to Church..192
Where Is the Monkey?..192

11 Coping in the Crisis...195
11-21 Years...195
Crisis Can Bring You Together 195
Divorce..195
Teenage Depression and Suicide 196
Legal Problems 197
    Drinking..198
    Drugs 198
When a Teenager Refuses...199
Gangs 200
Sex for the Wrong Reasons 200
If Your Daughter Is Pregnant 201
    Adoption...201
    Keeping the Baby...202
    Marriage 202
Dropping Out of School 202
Looking Back 203

12 Challenges to Your Plans 205
Single Parenthood 205
Differences in Kids...206
Birth Order Personality..206
    Oldest Children 207
    Firstborn Girls..208

Firstborn Boys 208
    Middlers Are Moderates 209
    The Baby Syndrome 210
Age-Spread Differences 211
Emotional Stress 211
    Experiences with Death 211
    Moving 212
    Handicaps 212
Temperamental Differences 213
What Is Hyperactivity? 213
Don't Jump to Conclusions 214
Should Hyper Kids Be Medicated? 215
Hyper with a Message 215
Consistency Calms Kids 216
Putting Differences to Use 216
Different Kids, Same Needs 217
Postscript **221**

CHAPTER 1
A Common Sense Starting Place

NEWS FLASH: "PERFECT PARENTS Produce Miserable Kids." Would you believe that our children learn more from how we handle our mess-ups, failures, and problems than they do from observing us doing everything perfectly?

Roger and I have a friend who almost waited too late to learn this lesson. He grew up with a father who seemed to be missing most of the time. When the father was present our friend learned mostly about what made his dad angry. So when this young man became a father himself, he vowed he would be "perfect." After years of failures and constant parenting guilt, our friend finally sought counseling. During one session, the counselor asked, "If you actually were to become the perfect parent, why would your kids need God?" It was a breakthrough moment for this guilt-ridden father, a flash of insight that freed a trapped man and broke a negative cycle. Now his children know why they need a perfect heavenly Father; their earthly father is far from perfect and always will be.

Learning from Your Own Parents' Imperfections

What have I learned from my own parents' imperfections? I've learned how to accept inconsistency. I've learned how to deal with errors in judgment. I've learned to respond to overreaction. I've learned that if you look hard enough, you can usually find a glimmer of humor in the imperfections. One thirteen year old told her father, "Sure, you knew all the state capitals when you were in junior high. There were only twenty states then!"

It's tough to find any humor when you have an alcoholic father, as I (Ron) did. Alcoholism is embarrassing. It was our family secret, we thought. During my grade school years I spent every free moment at other people's houses because I didn't want friends at my house, unless I knew my dad would be at work. By the time I reached junior high, my heart was filled with anger and resentment. My dad never physically abused me and he never belittled me; however, he did disappoint and confuse me regularly. I finally got to the point where I hated his bottle, I hated his slurred speech, and I hated him. Yet the more I expressed my bitterness, the more my father drank. Life seemed so unfair.

Why did Dad have to drink? Why couldn't we be like other families? Why couldn't he just stop? For the first twenty-five years of my life, Dad was an unconfessed alcoholic and the wall between us grew higher and wider. Christmas and Thanksgiving became extremely stressful. These holidays were supposed to be filled with joy and hope; for us, they were full of disappointment, heartache, and pain.

Until 1978 I was convinced that Dad had taught me nothing, that I had grown up cheated out of time and wisdom. Then the impossible happened. Dad checked himself into a treatment center, spent thirty-five days learning to be sober . . . and never drank again! We spent the next three years trying to forge a brand-new father/son relationship.

I suppose it wasn't until my dad died that I really got to know him. During what I considered thirty "wasted" years, God had poured some pretty important lessons into my life through my experiences with my father. But I had to let go of all the bitterness and resentment before I could see the good. In the painful hours of preparing for his funeral, I began remembering lessons I had never understood before:

Lesson One—Don't expect perfection. Every family has its secrets; no matter how good things look on the outside, there is always imperfection on the inside. Today we call it dysfunction. I spent the first thirty years of my life trying to be perfect in the hope that I could influence my dad to stop drinking. I wanted to be able to say the right thing at just the right time so he would stop.

I was fighting a losing battle because the Bible doesn't give us even one example of perfect human parents. All parents in the Bible failed—some messed up royally. God gave us principles to live by and then He provided a way to recover from our constant failure to live up to those principles. My dad's whole life taught me that truth.

Lesson Two—Don't freeze-frame anyone. Dad took home movies as we were growing up. On the evening of his funeral we watched the old reels for hours. We cried a little and laughed a lot. The experience was emotional, cathartic, healing, and unforgettable. We felt transported back in time as we relived those moments captured in the pictures, but when the reel was finished each of us realized that life keeps going. We were not the people trapped forever on that film. We were all older and wiser, living lives far more complicated than our lives of the past. We weren't what we used to be, and that was good.

Parents have a tendency to label or peg children—this one's funny, this one's smart, this one needs extra help. Labeling is like pausing the videotape at one frame and using it to

21

describe the still-pictured person for the rest of his or her life. Once my dad quit drinking he needed to be around people who would give him the freedom to change, to be radically different than he had been for years and years. I learned, from his example, how to trust people until they gave me definite reasons to do otherwise. We all need the freedom to grow and change, and so do our kids.

Lesson Three—*Always consider your options.* As Dad spent those years trapped in alcoholism, the bottle seemed to be his only option. But following his stay at the treatment center, he made it his job to search out and find other options. "Have you thought about . . . ?" became a stock response from him. He had found option hunting an incredibly freeing pursuit.

Once in a while everyone feels as though the roof has just caved in; fear and debris hide our choices. I have learned it's best to trust God and seek His options first. I may be temporarily blinded; I may never have all the facts. God, however, does have a better vantage point, so I determine to follow His lead.

Surveying the Essential Skills

This book is designed to help you avoid painful, self-inflicted parenthood traps that work to limit your parenting options. It will help you develop a parenting style you can live with as you guide your children from wonder to wisdom. So what are the absolutely essential skills you'll need? They fall into these two broad categories: 1) providing support—encouraging success and accepting failure; and 2) setting limits—drawing the line and holding to it. Five of these essential skills fall on the support side, five fall on the control side, while one skill—listening—is uniquely necessary to both categories.

Listening is required for setting limits *and* providing support. Listening for the real messages hidden behind the words is the most important skill we will learn in our lifetimes. It requires patience, humility, curiosity, trust, vulnerability, courage, and self-control. We will spend a lifetime learning to listen.

Providing Support

✓**Bonding.** Every child needs to form a strong attachment to her parent. Bonding develops through physical contact and time with the parent in conversation and play. Parental eye contact, physical expressions of affection, and acts of trustworthiness create strong bond. Daily activities and conversation together help turn infant bonding into family loyalty.

✓**Blessing.** At the surface level, blessing is simply the parent's verbal recognition of the child's worth. At a deeper level, it comprises direct expressions of love and appreciation for the child: "Jimmy, I'm so glad you're my son." At a still deeper level, it means unconditional acceptance, even in the midst of deep parental disappointment. Regularly conferring blessing on a child bestows the gift of growing confidence.

✓**Consoling.** Consolation begins by hurting with the child, then seeking to understand the child's pain from his or her perspective. Sometimes this skill requires the parent to be present without saying a word. The consoling parent helps the hurting child find a way through the pain and disappointment no matter how long it takes.

✓**Forgiving.** Parents and children are bound to hurt and disappoint one another in the course of their lives together. These small hurts, if not resolved, can grow into resentments that will destroy mutual respect. The ability to ask for, and to grant, forgiveness is one of the most important life skills a child can learn.

✓**Storytelling.** Parents reveal themselves in the stories they tell. Telling about your past—the good times and bad—your struggles, hopes, and dreams helps your children identify with you. Reading good stories aloud makes your children aware of your warmth, values, and sense of humor. Storytelling is one of your most effective methods of teaching values and shaping character.

Setting Limits

✓**Teaching.** Being able to teach children what to do and say is a fundamental skill of parenting. All parents teach, but some have the gift of turning mediocre events into lasting lessons. Years later some of those lessons will be passed on to their grandchildren. Parents who take the time to teach domestic skills, working skills, people skills, etc., seem to raise children who are more satisfied with life.

✓**Guiding.** All children need to be instructed, shown, and trained. Guiding parents go beyond merely teaching what they know; they arrange hands-on experiences for their children. These parents put words and concepts into action through ushering children directly into the wonder of living and learning.

✓**Limiting.** In a society that emphasizes freedom and independence, setting limits might seem foreign. But we must learn to limit our children's activities for their own good. Deciding what's good for our children, and setting the rules our families will live by, is one of the toughest, most crucial aspects of parenting.

✓**Confronting.** This parenting skill helps children face the consequences of behaviors that go beyond the limits. Although confrontation may at times be heated, it is not to be abusive. Parents who confront children are like referees who define expectations and help players play by the rules, stay in bounds, and pay the penalties for violations. Without confrontation our children will not know security.

✓**Negotiating.** Children learn how to resolve conflict by watching their parents deal with it. As parents settle differences with spouses, friends, and relatives, children soak up the experience. By modeling the benefits of compromise, you'll equip your children with a valuable coping skill.

Every parent has both strengths and weaknesses related to each of these skills. Take some time to evaluate your own skill levels by answering these questions: 1. Which two skills are my strongest? 2. Which two skills are my weakest? 3. Do I have stronger limit-setting skills or support-providing skills? 4. How would my spouse answer the above questions? 5. Which skill do I need to strengthen the most?

Recognizing Your Parenting Style

Now that you've surveyed the essential parenting skills, it's time to discover how your skills, background, and personality work together to form your natural parenting style. From the day we were born, God used the influences of our own parents, our basic temperaments, and our everyday experiences to shape us into potential parents. Weaving all those things together in some mysterious way, He provides us with our own, unique parenting style. Thankfully, we don't have to spend time attempting to take on someone else's style.

Read through the parenting style descriptions below. First look for the one that seems to fit you best. Then go back and determine which style you would find the most foreign to your background and personality.

Boss

Being in charge comes naturally for these parents. They enjoy giving orders and watching everything work smoothly. For them, being second-guessed is a sign of disrespect. The home atmosphere is usually very businesslike and fast paced, unless someone stages an insurrection! These parents may be driven toward success, winning, and being responsible for others. They are more comfortable dealing with action plans than with feelings. Loving support and loyalty toward children is assumed, but rarely expressed directly in displays of affection.

At the extreme, parents with this style may fail to teach their children to make their own decisions, since children are expected simply to obey the decisions made for them. In a dysfunctional application of this style, these parents can become like prison guards who push the children to achieve the goals the parents want. From the children's perspective, every time this kind of boss-parent speaks, it's an order . . . a command . . . a demand.

Friend

These parents love to have fun. They like to be funny and social. They live for people, and they want to be popular. For them, secrets are meant to be shared and concerns will be aired openly. Affection is demonstrated openly too. These parents are most uncomfortable when challenged to take control and administer discipline—which makes them feel like "the bad guy." They may be accused of being temperamental and can get their feelings hurt easily. Sometimes these parents find it tough to let go of their children as they grow up.

It's possible for parents with this style unintentionally to deny their children the opportunity to become mature, responsible adults. They may begin doing whatever is necessary to keep the friendship alive, perhaps trying to provide their children with the love, attention, and possessions they themselves did not receive as children. The hidden message these parents might send their children is: "We've got to stay best friends. Your other friends can never love you as much as I do."

Provider

These kind, agreeable parents just roll with the punches. They put a high value on avoiding conflict. Their focus is on providing the physical needs of the family. Closeness will not characterize their family because independence is so highly valued. Children are expected to handle problems themselves. These parents have a tendency to focus on their own careers at the expense of the children's emotional needs. They may even be accused of neglect when they show little interest in making family time a priority.

Taken to the extreme, this parenting style makes extremely few demands on children's behavior. These parents might allow the children to set their own rules and regulate their own behaviors. Keeping a safe distance from any deep emotional connection, they may send the message: "You're not very important to me." The children won't feel free; they'll feel abandoned.

Nurturer

These parents are organized, thoughtful, compassionate, patient, and seriously dedicated to parenting. They have decided to make parenting a primary focus of their lives. They take their children on nature trips, teach them new skills, and encourage them to try new things. They are very comfortable showing support and affection and just as comfortable setting limits. In general, parents with this style demonstrate the ability to balance all of the parenting basics.

These parents can be a little nit-picking and overly structured at times. The main danger is that nurturers will become enmeshed with their children to the point that they "smother-love" them. Nurturers need to know when and how to pull back from involvement in order to let children be children and adults be adults.

Avoiding Three Common Sources of Frustration

Typically, the nurturer style above fits most parents' vision of the kind of parent they would *like* to be. Though this may be our ideal model, things don't always work out as we plan. Within seconds of determining to start afresh with a new parenting attitude, our best intentions crumble and frustration runs rampant. How do you cope with those devastating parenting frustrations? Think through these "big three" for a moment—

Frustration #1: Not enough time. Years ago, in her book *If*

God Gave Speeding Tickets, Martha Bolton described American life. With some minor adjustments, her description still fits:

Our lives seem to be permanently set in high gear. From the moment we wake up, we're driving the fast lane—with no speed bumps in sight.

We eat in a hurry. Frankly, I don't think I've chewed my food since the spring of 1970. And I'm not saying how often I go to fast-food restaurants, but the other day I caught myself ordering into my mailbox and driving around the house.

We work in a hurry. We have computers, FAX machines, call waiting, beepers—and that's just for our preschoolers.

Sometimes we even pray in a hurry. We bow our heads and bring them up so fast we get whiplash.

This is the age of instant breakfasts, sixty-second hair conditioners and drive-thru surgical centers. Even our photo developing is fast. Now we can get our vacation pictures back and start boring our friends within thirty minutes.

But why all the rush? Why not take a moment to let the coffee percolate? Why not tap the brakes a little and reevaluate what's really important in life? Our only free day shouldn't be February 29. And our only stroll down the boulevard shouldn't be when we run out of gas taking the kids to school. After all, the world God created isn't spinning any faster. Why should his children?

We dream of freezing time, borrowing time, and saving time, but these dreams are illusions. All children ever want is "five more minutes," and we act as though we have the power to grant such a request. Time seems to be the money of the 1990s. That's why we always want more.

Frustration #2: Losing Control. When 150 nine to twelve

28

year olds were asked what they disliked most about their mothers, the response was overwhelming. Over and over the children said, "I can't stand it when she loses it—when she screams."

Women scream; men yell. Either way, it's a sign of losing control.

An unknown observer of life in the 1990s has concluded that we are aware of the needs of more people, empathize with a greater number of tribulations, join more causes, confront more potential threats and enemies, sustain more social obligations, experience more longings and disappointments, and are tempted by more varied and tantalizing possibilities than ever before.

Does this turmoil sound familiar? Tommy needs to eat at 6:00 P.M. because of a school function at 7:00. His sister, Joy, must be picked up from her volleyball game at 7:15. Both children are upset because Mom has to attend an office function and can't get home until 8:15, thus no dinner and no transportation. Mom asks Dad to come to the rescue, but he has to work late to prepare for a flight to Chicago the next morning. To complicate matters, it's Grandma's birthday tomorrow, and Mom hasn't bought her present yet. There is an urgent message on the answering machine from a longtime friend of the family, who is in town and wants to drop by for the evening. And one of Mom's friends has left a tearful message about her unraveling marriage. The bills have been collecting in the "bill drawer" for forty-five days, the house is a wreck, both cars need an oil change—and Mom and Dad have a nagging feeling they have forgotten something!

Seems to me, losing control once in a while may be more healthy than constantly struggling to keep it. Either way, our balance is shot.

Frustration #3: This isn't working. Have you ever wondered why it is that when people talk about their vacations, invariably they take great pleasure in sharing what went wrong? Lost luggage, flat tires, surprise mishaps, embarrassing moments, and minor misfortunes dominate the whole conversation. When talking about parenting experiences, parents also tend to concentrate on what isn't working. Why is that?

For years Ron has been a guest on a national television call-in counseling program. Over the years, thousands of people have called the show seeking advice. They share their problem, Ron gets clarification and then offers some suggestions. The listener's most common response is, "I tried that. It won't work." The truth is, these callers don't really want help; they want to tell us why things won't work in order to justify everything they have done. They are seeking approval for their failures.

When our focus is on our frustration, it is impossible to be a nurturing parent. Until we get back in balance, the best discipline methods in the world won't do a bit of good.

Adjusting Your Personal Balance

We love the following definition of insanity: "To do the same thing over and over again, expecting different results." Yet there are proven steps that can help parents avoid "insanity" and regain a sense balance, regardless of their natural parenting style. Consider these five suggestions for handling a typical parenting "crisis":

1. Close your eyes and take four uninterrupted deep breaths.

2. Spend a few moments in prayer. Confess your readiness to overreact. Confess your frustration. Ask God to help you regain your balance and to grow from the experience.

3. Identify a parenting skill that will help you deal with the present situation. Make sure it's one of your strengths.

4. Ask yourself, "What will my child learn from this?"

5. Ask yourself, "What have I learned from this?"

Based on your background, your personality, and your adult

experiences, you have a natural parenting style. Is there something you would like to change about your style? Ask God to help you work on one skill at a time. Then trust God, not your own ability. Write your request on a card and keep the card with you at all times. Read it daily. Then wait for God to act. Remember that He works on His schedule, not yours.

CHAPTER 2
The Basics of Common Sense Discipline

THE POPULAR MISCONCEPTION IS that discipline means punishment. That's obvious when we hear a parent tell a child, "You'd better straighten up, or I'm going to lay some discipline on you." What Dad really means is, "Stop that, or you're going to get it." However, the English word "discipline" comes from the Latin *disciplina,* which means "to instruct." The word for discipline in the New Testament has the same root as disciple, or learner. Discipline, in any language, primarily involves teaching and learning.

Throughout the Bible we see God using the discipline process in three ways. In Moses' sermon text of Deuteronomy 8:1-5, for instance, God is portrayed as a father who 1) leads (the process that prevents misbehavior); humbles (the process that designs consequences for not keeping His commands); and tests (the process that redeems the habitually defiant or rebellious). God was preparing His children for life then, and He is still preparing them today.

Jesus' followers were called "disciples" because they dedicated their whole lives to learning from Jesus. If you want to effectively discipline your child, think of discipline as preparation for living a grown-up life. Instead of asking, "What's the best way to discipline my child?" we might do better by asking, "What do I want my child to learn from this? How can I teach my child to become a loving, responsible adult in the same way God is teaching me?"

Responsibility: The Common Sense Goal

In this generation you could drive yourself crazy trying to be a good parent based on what the experts say. Many parents would do better by forgetting the textbooks and the theories and learning to relax a little. And nothing will help you enjoy the adventure of parenting more than learning how to be more comfortable and confident in your approach to discipline.

The primary goal of common sense discipline is to help parents raise resourceful children who will become responsible adults. This discipline process takes each child down the path from wonder to wisdom. The goal is worthy, but it calls for a major investment of parental time, energy, and patience. Finding themselves short on one or more those items, some parents quit before they really get started. We hope you won't.

The Discipline Chart on the following page describes the process of helping your child become responsible. Both parent and child will have to take this journey together. As the kids grow older, they are encouraged to make their own decisions and control their own behavior. The process is like teaching your child to ride a bicycle. At first you hold the bike steady and run alongside for at least a thousand miles. As your child gets his balance, you turn loose for a while. Then, after dozens of scraped knees and a few minor emergencies, your child becomes a certified, safe bicycle rider—as you look on, beaming with pride.

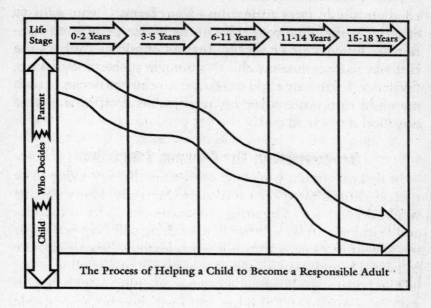

Life Stage	0-2 Years	3-5 Years	6-11 Years	11-14 Years	15-18 Years

The Process of Helping a Child to Become a Responsible Adult

Using the Discipline Chart as a guide, let's consider some of the issues in the life of a developing child. For example, during the 0-2 years, parents will make all the decisions for their children. The only exception might be to let the child select some of her toys.

During the 3-5 years, parents will make most of the decisions for their children, especially in the health and safety areas. So, in the second column we might imagine a parent who decides whether or not her child will go to day care, Sunday school, or no preschool at all. That decision is completely up to the parent. The child's choices might be limited to such things as deciding what to take for "show and tell." When your four year old makes a request, ask yourself: "Should I decide this, or should she decide?"

While your child is 6-11 years old, you'll still want to make

35

most of the major decisions about schooling. However, only your child can decide how he will relate to other kids at school. During this time we encourage parents to permit children to decide what clothes to wear to school. Getting a little chilly because he wore a short-sleeve shirt instead of a long-sleeve shirt will cause a child to make a better decision next time. (As Ron was growing up he often wondered why he had to put on his coat when his mother got cold. How about you?)

During the 11-14 years, statements such as these might be appropriate: "Homework is now your responsibility. If you need help, I'll help, if I can. If your grades start to suffer, then your activities will be cut back, and you'll have a scheduled study time."

In the years from 15-18, parents with common sense discipline really make very few decisions for their teens. Their teens will mess up, but they'll get good parental advice and learn how to repair the damage. They practice being responsible.

Some parents may object to this guide and say it's too permissive or even irresponsible. Not so. Remember that the goal is *not* blind obedience. The goal is to help resourceful children become loving, responsible adults. Like removing braces once the teeth are straight, there comes a time when the tight corrective structure has to be gradually and carefully removed.

Throughout this book we'll refer to the Discipline Chart to point out appropriate discipline methods. We will also use the chart to reflect on how difficult it is, at times, for parents to let the kids take responsibility for their own decisions.

Negative Attention: A Motive for Misbehavior

Rudolph Dreikurs, an expert in child psychology and classroom discipline, has identified four goals children often seek by their misbehavior. The following chart can be helpful to you in responding when your child misbehaves.

Let's focus on the first motive for misbehavior, negative

Why Do They Do That?

Child's Actions	Parent's/ Teacher's Reaction	The Child's Goal	Options For Parents/Teachers
Nuisance Clown Lazy	Irritated Constant reminding and occasional yelling	Attention (Negative attention)	• Avoid giving negative attention. • Catch 'em being good • Affirm the child • **Use time-out for punishment**
Stubborn Argues Tells lies Disobedient	Angry Feels provoked and threatened	Taking control (Trying to lead)	• Refuse to argue • Let the child know that "he may be right" • Talk (later) about what's happening. • **Use negative practice for punishment**
Vicious Revengeful Lashes out	Hurt Tendency to retaliate	Retaliation (Payment for past hurt)	• Look for ways to encourage • Avoid the hurt reaction • **Use consequences for punishment**
Hopeless Helpless Gives up Loner	Give up Nothing seems to work	Keep from trying (If I don't try, I can't fail)	• Encourage efforts, not performance • Use reinforcement and incentives • Stop all criticism • **Focus on strengths**

attention. If we think a child is continually acting up just to get us to notice, he is probably trying to do just that. Since any attention the child gets for acting up may simply encourage more acting up, it can become a vicious cycle. The child acts up to get negative attention, we scold and punish the child, so he's reinforced by getting the negative attention, and the misbehavior intensifies. Then we try avoiding the child because he's so obnoxious. We then start feeling guilty. The child, feeling ignored and unwanted, seeks more attention. By this time he may have forgotten how to get positive attention, or may have decided that negative attention is easier to get, so he simply does the same thing he did before and acts up again. And the cycle goes round and round.

Attention to a child is like water to a thirsty person. Imagine being stranded, without hope of rescue, having gone without water for days. By chance you find a polluted pool. Aware of the danger, you drink anyway to stay alive. Really desperate people will do almost anything to meet their needs.

Children who are desperate for attention may do desperate things to get it. When children are quite small, they naturally get lots of attention just for being babies, all cute and cuddly. After a while many kids stop getting as much attention as they'd like, so they just continue acting like a baby. It may "work" for a while, but it always makes things worse. Negative attention doesn't satisfy as positive attention does. If children aren't getting enough positive attention, they'll get attention of one sort or another, one way or the other. That's why many kids seem to act up on purpose even when it's obvious they're about to be punished.

Children who are continually ignored by a parent can become emotionally neglected and severely depressed. At times their need for attention may be so great that they will deliberately goad the guilty parent to the point of child abuse. They know that after the abuse takes place, the parent's next actions will usually include some sort of attention, if only out of guilt.

In a similar fashion, it's not uncommon for some teenage girls to become sexually involved with boys as a substitute for the normal attention and affection they should be receiving from their fathers. Unfortunately, things often get out of control, and some of these girls wind up pregnant. That's one sure way finally to get Dad's attention, but the price is far too high.

If your child has been acting up and you suspect he's trying to get negative attention, before responding with the typical gripe-out session or an unnecessary spanking, talk openly about your observation and share how you feel about the situation. One father said it like this: "If you want my attention, that isn't the way to go about getting it. What you're doing just gets me angry. Now let's talk about what you want." His child said "Okay" and then Dad stated, "I'll be glad to give you some attention if you'll tell me just what you want."

It helps to talk about the situation with the child. The key for parents is to listen and be aware of what's really going on under the surface. Look for the hidden message behind the behavior. Use open discussion to help the child change his pattern and break the habit of seeking attention through misbehavior.

Values: The Character-Development Challenge

Ron asked hundreds of seminar participants to write down the number-one value they wanted their children to have when they left home. The overwhelming response was: honesty. Personal faith, sexual morality, compassion, and kindness rounded out the top five. What would your response be?

The way we discipline our children will determine what values they take with them when they leave home. If character means having the courage to live out our values, then what we all need is a large dose of character. In his book *The Moral Life of Children*, Dr. Robert Coles describes character as: "Moral firmness, the ability to respond to setbacks, the willingness to deny personal desires for the good of the group, the development of a wholesome sense of humor that allows one to see that there is more to life than living. And the ability to accept others as individuals, even though they may be very different."

We all want our children to be honest, reliable, fair, self-controlled, and respectful. But *wanting* our children to have these traits and actually *instilling* them are two very different things. We seem to be uncertain about how to develop character in our children. Do we parents really make a difference anymore?

Some experts believe that all our societal problems would

39

be solved if we could just raise self-esteem levels among children. These experts define behavior problems as the natural result of certain unmet psychological needs. The "old-fashioned" idea that most behavior problems are the result of sheer willfulness on the part of children doesn't occur to this new wave of child experts. Besides, we cannot develop self-esteem in children simply by telling them, over and over, how great they are. We develop self-esteem by giving children opportunities to be accountable and responsible. (It's worth noting that a study of child-rearing articles in *Ladies Home Journal*, *Woman's Home Companion*, and *Good Housekeeping* for the years 1890, 1900, and 1910 found that one-third of the articles were about how to help children develop the courage to live out their values—instilling character in children.)

An old WWII story has surfaced again in the 1990s. It seems a naval destroyer was assigned the duty to patrol the Atlantic coastline of America, protecting against German submarines. It was a foggy night, and the captain noticed a light ahead. He instructed his signalman to have the ship ahead change course by ten degrees. The message came back, "You should change your course."

The puzzled captain sent another message, "I am the captain. You change *your* course." The response was, "I am a Seaman 2nd Class; change your course."

They were getting dangerously close, so the captain sent one more message: "This is a US destroyer; change your course now." The return message was short and effective: "This is the lighthouse; change your course."

We need a lighthouse for the nineties. Our children are desperate for a solid sense of right and wrong and the courage to choose the right. Addressing the 1987 graduating class of Duke University, Ted Koppel of ABC's "Nightline" suggested that the Bible be considered as the source of our core values.

In the place of truth, we have discovered facts.

For moral absolutes, we have substituted moral ambiguity. We now communicate with everyone and say absolutely nothing. We have reconstructed the Tower of Babel, and it is a television antenna: a thousand voices producing a daily parody of democracy, in which everyone's opinion is afforded equal weight regardless of substance or merit. Indeed, it can even be argued that opinions of real weight tend to sink with barely a trace in television's ocean of banalities. What Moses brought down from Mt. Sinai were not the Ten Suggestions. They are commandments. *Are*, not *were*. The sheer brilliance of the Ten Commandments is that they codify in a handful of words acceptable human behavior, not just for then or now, but for all time.

All the great events and personalities of the Old and New Testaments teach us the values of truth, justice, and mercy. In some cases, real people face real consequences when they fail to honor the truth. Those stories exemplify discipline in action.

We may not agree on all the values that should be taught, but we should all agree on basic character traits such as honesty, courage, respect for the rights of others, and responsibility. Parents across this country are making it clear that they want their children to learn a personal sense of right and wrong. They want the "little voice" inside their children to speak up and speak out.

Family Health: What Can We Do?

Remember, it is the goal of common sense discipline to help parents raise resourceful children who grow into responsible adults. This process is far more comprehensive than becoming proficient in the latest discipline techniques. Merely resorting to punishment when the rules are broken can become a cold

41

and mechanical drudgery. Placing discipline in the context of teaching and training, however, gives new life to the whole process.

The power of common sense discipline doesn't come from the quick mastery of new techniques. The power comes from the heart and soul of parents who care about the behavior, the values, the character, and the eternal destiny of their children. To recharge that power source daily, we must be vigilant about keeping our families healthy. Here are three suggestions that can help.

1. Define your family's purpose. The family needs a stronger unifying principle than "making each other happy." The family needs a purpose beyond itself, a calling that requires self-denial, serving others, or helping the helpless. When parents decide what their family stands for, then discipline problems will diminish and character will return. The focus will be on teaching, not crisis management.

2. Put God at the center. National research has consistently declared that strong families have a sense of religious devotion. We must return tradition and ritual to our families. Sadly, the only daily ritual practiced regularly in American households is the ritual of watching television.

3. Revive the practice of family reading. Don't stop reading together when the kids are old enough to read for themselves. Your conversations will be more lively and interesting than any TV program. And family time will become inspirational rather than merely therapeutic.

CHAPTER 3
Showing Love and Support

EVEN INCONSISTENT AND SOMEWHAT harsh discipline will work, if your children know you love them unconditionally. Unconditional love is an "in spite of . . ." kind of love; it's accepting your child the way she is, no matter how disappointed you are in your child's behavior and no matter what handicaps she has or what she looks like. The rub is that most parents today have no idea what this unconditional love feels like or looks like because they have never experienced it themselves. So this chapter describes the kinds of things parents are doing when expressing unconditional love in practical ways.

Modeling Values

Children learn a lot from watching others. We've all seen children trying to walk like their daddy, make friends like their mother, or yell like someone down the street. "Monkey see, monkey do" is the hallmark of all small children.

Anthropologist Deborah Tannen has written a revealing book about the differences between men and women. She contends that women focus on talking to develop intimacy and understanding, while men focus on solving problems and sharing information. Men tend to be more silent, while women tend to be more talkative. Many men may consider discussing feelings unnecessary, while women consider talk about feelings as a first step toward understanding and rapport. Men are more inclined to give information than praise. Women, on the other hand, are more inclined to give praise than information. Men experience life as a contest, a struggle to preserve independence and avoid failure. Women approach the world as a growing connection of individuals—a network.

Our children grow up in a house with two very different individuals who are trying in their own ways to demonstrate love and affection. Like sponges, our children soak up every detail related to how we treat each other, how we argue, how we solve problems, how we deal with failure, how we confess and forgive. In short, they find in our lives a live-in portrayal of unconditional love in action. And our actions always speak louder than our words.

One father complained to Roger that his son was rude and ill-mannered toward his mother. When Roger observed the family together he realized that the boy learned rudeness from the way his father treated his mother. If we resort to saying, "Do as I say, and not as I do," then our words become cheap; we lose integrity and authority in our parenting leadership.

How soon do children start modeling the actions of those around them? Roger tells about a funny incident that his wife, Kathy, pointed out to him. Kathy said, "Roger, you know that funny way you curl your little finger when you hold a cup of tea? Watch how Lane holds his orange-juice glass at breakfast tomorrow."

Lane was two years old then. Sure enough, he held his hand the same way I did, purposefully curling his little finger. I even

3 Showing Love and Support

caught him looking at the way I held my knife and fork while he tried to copy me. Don't underestimate modeling as an effective communicator of love.

Exploring New Worlds

Once, when Roger's son Lane was four years old, they were sitting by a shallow fountain in the center of a shopping mall, and Lane was pushing a small boat around the circular pool. Soon another little boy about Lane's age came over, and they began taking turns with the boat. While the other boy was pushing the boat through the water, Lane decided to get up on the concrete ledge that went all the way around the fountain. This ledge was about one foot wide and two feet off the mall's floor. Roger was tempted to tell him to get down because he might slip, but, on second thought, he decided to wait and see what would happen. Besides, walking around the ledge of a fountain looked like fun.

Roger felt some risk in letting Lane do what he was doing. The ledge was concrete, and there were some slippery places on it where the water had splashed. So he considered the worst thing that could happen: Lane might slip and bump his head. Then Roger thought about what would happen if he told Lane, "No, you can't do that. Get down, come here, etc." Lane would beg to continue trying to walk the ledge, giving endless reassurances that he could do it.

Roger didn't think it was likely that Lane would have a bad fall, but there was a real possibility that he might get soaked. Fortunately, it was a warm day, and Lane was wearing shorts, so getting wet wasn't a big problem. Roger decided that if Lane did fall, he would learn a lesson that would probably have a lasting impact, so without comment he let Lane continue to walk around the ledge. Kids do love fountains, and Lane was only doing a perfectly natural thing for a kid.

Well, Lane didn't fall in. In fact, he jumped in! Later, a man who had been watching everything from the other side of the fountain told Roger that it was obvious when Lane got the idea. "It was written all over his face; he just squatted down and jumped in," the man said. In all fairness to Lane, his version was that he was about to slip, and rather than lose his balance and fall, he chose to jump.

Lane came out of the water in near panic. Naturally, his first concern was Roger's reaction.

"Are you okay?" Roger asked.

Lane nodded.

"That was really something!" Roger continued.

Again Lane nodded.

"I guess that water was really wet!" Roger offered. "Do you have any fish in your pockets?"

Now, there are many good parents who would have "put their foot down" and told their child to get off that ledge. Some kids would obey immediately and that would be the end of it. But many good children, upon hearing such a statement, would have firmly decided, "The first chance I get, I will get on that ledge . . . when Mom or Dad aren't around."

Most of us have had the experience of saying, "I want to try it my way!" or, "Let me try it myself!" When we allow and even encourage our children to explore safe ways of doing new things, we provide them the opportunity to make useful and lasting discoveries. We also demonstrate, in a powerful way, how much we love them.

Questioning and Reflecting

Questions aren't always for the purpose of getting information. Sometimes they're intended to begin an adventure that leaves us more confident of our love and more understanding of each other. Some great adventures have begun with the following questions:

Are we there yet?

Why can't I unburn my finger?

How many bites of this stuff do I have to eat?

Can you read that story again?

When leaves fall off trees, why do they get rusty?

How come my reflection is left handed?

Why don't you just get more money from the hole in the wall?

What's eternity mean?

Questions do get our attention, but we can have too much of a good thing. Sometimes this questioning routine will go on until we get tired and angry (somewhere between questions number three and number ten). Then in frustration we bark, "Just because!" "Go ask Dad!" "That's enough; go look it up for yourself!" "That's it; I don't want to hear another word!" And the request for adventure fades for the moment.

How can we use questions effectively? The next time a child asks you three questions in a row, you might pretend you are playing a child's version of "20 Questions." Instead of responding to question number four too readily, it might be useful to think about what's going on and how you could use this situation as a teaching opportunity. Shift gears and say something like, "Hmm, that's a good question. I bet if you stop to think about it you can come up with the answer yourself." Or, "What do you think the answer could be?"

In one family Ron worked with, Dad liked to order his kids: "Go look it up yourself." His wanted to encourage his children to become resourceful and more independent. Unfortunately, he accomplished just the opposite by the sarcastic way he responded to their questions. Soon they didn't bother to ask him anything of importance out of fear that he would reject them.

What would have happened to that father's relationship with his children if the next time he was asked a question he offered to look up the answer *with* the questioner? He could

have said: "That's a good question. Let's look it up together."
He could have used the child's question as an opportunity to
explain ways of finding solutions by saying something like,
"Let's see, the best place to find out the meaning of a word is
in the dictionary. The best place to find out more about those
words is in an encyclopedia. Let's see if this one has it. Now,
how is that word spelled?" And so his child would spell the
word for him. "Okay, this book is in alphabetical order, so we
use it like this." The child learns a useful lesson while having
his sense of being loved confirmed in a practical way.

If the question is about life, it's a great opportunity to discuss personal beliefs and values. These times can become significant memories for the kids. Notice that questions can be
very useful in helping us invest our time in our children's lives.
They are a natural opportunity to show we care.

Empowering

Some time ago Roger was visiting friends whose children he
had never met. As He drove up, out came George and Gracie's
two sons, ages six and three. When Roger got out of the car
George's oldest son introduced himself and said, "Hi, I'm Billy
and this is my brother, Bobby. He's shy." Bobby, who had been
smiling until that remark, promptly hung his head.

"Hi, Bobby. How are you?" No response from Bobby.

About that time George came out and said, "Hi, Roger,
have you met the kids? This is our oldest, Billy, and here's
Bobby; he's the shy one."

We all walked inside and George's father greeted Roger and
asked if he had met everybody. "Here's Billy and there's Bobby.
He's shy."

Incredible! Roger had been there less than five minutes and
already three generations of Bobby's family had told him that
Bobby was shy. Roger says, "Wherever you are, Bobby, my
hat's off to you, pal. You are a neat little guy, but you're going

to need lots of other voices to counteract those three. I doubt that you started off feeling shy, but it's easy to see what *keeps* you feeling that way."

We can empower our children to become what we predict. We can use positive statements to encourage and affirm them. By actually saying the words, we empower our children to reach beyond their limitations. Try phrases like:

Now you've got it!

You catch on fast!

It's great living with a kid like you!

You're on the right track!

This is super!

You really stick to it!

You're doing much better!

That's your best ever!

Aren't you proud of the way you've improved?

You're getting better every day!

I am really pleased with what you did!

Isn't it great to be finished?

I am proud of you!

Top notch!

Wow, you certainly used your time wisely!

You can do it by yourself now!

Children warm to such statements and find them reassuring. Kids rarely hear too much of this kind of affirmation from their parents.

Twice in the New Testament God spoke publicly about His Son, once at Jesus' baptism and again at His Transfiguration. Here's what God said after Jesus was baptized, "This is my Son, whom I love; with him I am well pleased" (Matt. 3:17). God repeated that affirmation at the Transfiguration, adding, "Listen to him!" (Matthew 17:5). If God found it necessary to say the words, shouldn't we do likewise?

How many times have you heard a parent say in front of

friends or strangers, "This is our daughter. We're very proud of her"? What do people hear you say about your child?

Playing

Playing with our children may be the most important thing we can do to show we love them. Playing gives us the chance to demonstrate our love and learn a lot about our children at the same time. When your child is young, try one or more of the play activities listed below. You will find yourself connecting on a feeling level. When playing, the emphasis should be on being, not doing.

Water Play. Playing in a tub of warm water stimulates inhibited children and soothes explosive children. A warm bath may help relieve stress, if you can get him or her in the tub.

Modeling clay. Kids can mold clay to express feelings of fear, anger, sadness, or joy. Say: "Make something that looks like how you feel."

Painting. Children paint what they feel or what matters in their lives. Finger painting is a good medium for such expression of moods.

Puzzles. Working puzzles helps children to create order out of chaos. Children whose lives have become disoriented, confused, or disrupted will often feel better after putting a puzzle together.

Toys. Children take on different roles, depending on the toys they use. Often the victim becomes the rescuer, the one who calls the shots.

Puppets. Children become talkative and expressive with puppets. Puppets are always good listeners.

Books. Kids may not have the vocabulary to express their feelings. Books can help them share both positive and negative feelings.

Cuddle Toys. Sitting quietly with a cuddly toy can soothe

an angry or fearful child. Some teachers use a stuffed dog as a stress-management tool in the classroom.

Music. Listening to music is a wonderful way to release tension. As children get older, music becomes an appropriate escape—a safe, private world.

Informal Play. Active play allows for release of emotional energy in an appropriate way, while quiet games may be comforting to a child who chooses to be alone.

When the children get older, playing catch, going camping, attending a sporting event, and playing video games are examples of play activities that communicate love.

Comforting in Failure

Comforting a child doesn't mean solving all their problems, or fixing things when they break. Comforting starts with feeling what the child is feeling. One young girl was spending some time shopping with her father. They enjoyed the day together, but at the last moment the little girl asked permission to go get ice cream. Warning her to be back at the car on time, the tired father granted the girl's request.

The little girl lost track of time and hadn't returned promptly. Now Dad would be late for his appointment. He was furious. Finally, the little girl got back to the car, but without the ice cream.

Dad looked straight into her watery eyes and asked, "Where have you been? You know I was in a hurry!"

"I'm sorry, Daddy," the repentant girl replied. "But Jenny was there, and her doll broke."

Calmed a bit, Dad said, "And so you helped her fix her doll?" The little girl answered, "No, I helped her cry." Sometimes we think our best response to a hurting child is to cure instead of care. We want to fix instead of feel. Many times we miss the point. By feeling first we show our love in unforgettable ways.

51

Hugging and Touching

Years ago I discovered *The Hug Therapy Book* (CompCare Publications, 1983). It's a wonderful little book by Kathleen Keating. It has changed my view of hugs. Hugs help both the hugger and the hug-ee to open doors to feelings, ease tension, slow down aging, keep shoulder muscles in condition, and dispel loneliness. Hugging, according to Keating, "Makes impossible days possible, fills up empty places in our lives, and keeps on working to dispense benefits even after the hug's released."

Keating suggests, "To keep little ones from growing up thinking that hugs are only for sexual intimacy, hug them often—affectionately, supportively, playfully, and tenderly. Let them see parents and other adults hugging in these ways. Otherwise they may grow up believing that hugs are for lovers only, and that in order to be hugged—and huggable—one must be physically attracted to the other hugger."

Sometimes a simple touch may speak louder than any words. Touch has been proven to encourage positive feelings about ourselves and our circumstances, help premature babies confined to an incubator to grow and thrive, and have a positive effect on the development of a child's IQ.

Demonstrating Love

For children raised in loving and supportive homes, love is expressed in many different words and actions. It won't take long for parents to find the "language" that suits them best. For some, just saying the words "I love you" will be very difficult. They will want their actions to demonstrate how they feel. Actions do speak loudly, but without the words to give the actions meaning and definition, kids are left free to misinterpret the actions. And with just the words to go on, kids may never *feel* loved, even though they know they are. Without the foundation of an atmosphere of unconditional love, children have a tendency to grow up searching for love, feeling defective, limited in their ability to be intimate with another human being.

CHAPTER 4
Setting Limits and Controlling Behavior

ROGER, NOTHING SEEMS TO WORK with this kid of mine. I've tried everything—spanking, grounding, sending him to his room. I feel like a failure. I think it's hopeless." Can you identify with that? Roger hears words like those frequently.

Roger explains,

"A while back I got a sore throat and started looking in the medicine cabinet for something to take. After searching I found some pills left from a previous trip to the doctor for the same problem, so I took those for three days and felt much better. Three days later the sore throat came right back, worse this time, so I called the doctor's office. When I told his nurse what had happened and what medication I had taken, she started laughing. Her laughter embarrassed me; I've never been altogether comfortable being laughed at. This time I learned firsthand that you have to take the right medication, and it takes a full seven days to do the trick."

Discipline works a lot like medicine. Sometimes you have to keep giving discipline until the job is done. Many different kinds of discipline work fine if you will use them long enough. Too many parents stop using good discipline measures before they can take effect.

The Triangle Perspective

Roger encourages parents to think of discipline in a "triangle" perspective. Parents set rules and guidelines that are matched with appropriate consequences and limits, all within an atmosphere of high expectation and unconditional acceptance. As the children grow older, provide decreasing amounts of protection as they grow more competent, while at the same time increasing the amounts of consequences needed to keep them in bounds. The triangle perspective will help you prepare for the day when our children are released from our control—their "Independence Day."

This chapter describes discipline techniques. There are four common sense techniques that can be readily adapted to each child or situation. We will add spanking as crisis technique. In fact, God uses these four methods in disciplining His children. All four methods can be used effectively during the first eleven or so years. The first two methods are more appropriate for teen years (11-18). Here are the methods:

1. Catch 'em doing something right,
2. Logical consequences,
3. Time-out,
4. Negative practice.

Catch 'Em Doing Something Right

It takes time to make any kind of discipline work. It's the kind of love God showed His Son when He said, "This is my beloved Son." It's the kind of discipline God showed the children of Israel as He led them out of Egypt and reminded them of His presence in a pillar of cloud by day and fire by night (Exodus13:21) and when He fed them manna (Exodus 16).

The Power of a Positive Word

These days most of the reminders kids hear focus on their problems. Kids hear about their mistakes from everyone. Think how much better off children would be if they heard positive reminders that regardless of their failures, they are moving in the right direction.

Roger explains,

> The meanest kid I ever knew was William. He was twelve years old, and his home was like a combat zone. His parents had lots of problems, and William had absorbed many of them. Placed in a camp for disturbed children where Kathy (my wife) and I were counselors, William sought to test and break every rule he could. At first he did a pretty good job of it. I said he was ornery; he was also obnoxious, as obnoxious as they come.
>
> On one particularly rough day with William, it struck me that about ninety percent of the attention he received from adults was for his misbehavior. Yet even at his worse he was only ornery about ten percent of the time. The rest of the time he was either neutral or acceptable. Yet the bulk of his attention from adults focused on the small percentage of his misbehavior.
>
> So Kathy and I started looking for positive things to say about William. At first we had to look long and hard, but you usually find what you look for, and so did we. We started telling William when he was doing OK and some of the things we liked about him. We didn't unload all at once because, after all, we didn't want him to get whiplash. The more we talked about positives, the more there were to talk

about. Slowly, like a huge ship turning, William
started coming around.

Start Right Now

What would happen if right now you put this book down
and caught your children doing something right? What would
they do if you told them how pleased you were? Would they
pass out from shock and surprise? Why don't you try it? Take
a chance! If they're small, they'll probably eat it up. If they're
teenagers, they'll probably act embarrassed. Don't make a big
deal of it, just say something like, "I appreciate the way you're
trying." Or, "I know school is tough right now with all the
pressures, and I want you to know that I care about you and I
believe in you." Who knows? If it worked for William, it can
work for you too.

Speaking up about the good things shows you're thinking
about the good that's present in all children. It's accentuating
the positive. When was the last time you surprised your children with an "I love you" statement? Do you like "I love you"
statements? What would happen if you started to sprinkle a
few compliments here and there? You'll never know for sure
until you try.

The "Boss" and "Provider" parenting style have the most
difficulty with catching children doing things right. The
"Nurturer" and "Friend" styles find it easy.

Logical Consequences

Dr. Rudolph Dreikurs is usually associated with popularizing
the concept of logical consequences with children. In Scripture
logical consequences are described by God throughout Exodus
21-23. There God outlines a number of rules and the consequences for breaking them. If the rule was broken accidentally
(Exodus 22:5) then repayment was based on an equal basis. If a
deliberate theft took place repayment might range from four to
five times the value of what was stolen (Exodus 22:1).

The term "logical consequence" comes from a logical relationship between what is expected and what takes place. Think of it as an "if/then" relationship. "If you don't . . . then you won't."

Consequences Speak Loudly

The value of logical consequences comes from permitting children to experience the results or consequences of their actions. For example, "If you continue to play with your milk, then it may spill. That will be all the milk you'll get for this meal." For logical consequences to work the parents must be willing to allow children to experience some unpleasant consequences, like doing without more milk, if the kids are to learn how life really works. Certainly you should never permit your child to risk any physical danger just to teach a lesson, but allowing an occasional bump or unpleasant experience will often teach far more than warnings or lectures.

Logical consequences can also have a positive result. For example, "If you continue to save your allowance, then you'll soon have enough to buy the CD you've been wanting."

Two general logical consequences are known as the grandparents' rules:

Grandma's Rule: "No ice cream until you eat your vegetables," or "You get to do what you want after you do what I want you to do."

Grandpa's Rule: "If you break it then you fix it," or "If you make a mess then you have to clean it up."

Roger's Rule: "If you want something extra then you will have to figure out how to get it," or "When your allowance is used up you'll have to find ways to make extra money."

Natural Consequences

Sometimes logical consequences occur naturally, without parents having to do anything out of the ordinary. For example,"If you leave your textbook outside the rain may ruin it, and then you will have to use your savings to pay for a new one." Most logical consequences are set up by parents using "if/then" wording which permits children to learn by experience.

You may have noticed that most children try to manipulate parents when first presented with logical consequences, "Oh, Mom, please, can't you wait just fifteen minutes longer?" If you let your child manipulate you then logical consequences won't work. If you let your children experience some disappointment as a result of their misbehavior they'll take you seriously next time. Many parents could save themselves a lot of anguish at mealtimes by simply telling children when dinner is ready and then sitting down to eat when it's served. Or they may call children in once and only once from playing, and then sit down to eat. If Junior comes in on time, then he'll have a hot meal with the rest of the family. If he doesn't, then he won't. I know it sounds harsh, but, believe me, it is not. It's teaching about life. How many parents do you know who call their children again and again, "Come in now, I said!"

Schedules and Promises

Many things in our lives operate by the standards of logical consequences. If we intend for our children to become competent in dealing with the workaday world, then it's vital for them to learn how to deal with the consequences. Schedules and promptness depend on logical consequences. So, "If you are ready when the school bus comes, then you'll get to ride it to school. If you aren't ready on time, then you'll probably miss the bus and be tardy." How many of you have remembered late Saturday afternoon that what you wanted to wear to church the next day was at the cleaner? Then you rushed to the cleaner only to arrive five minutes after they closed for the weekend. That's how it works in real life.

Fines and Penalties

Have you ever thought about how many fines and penalties there are in life? Overdue library books, late payments, cars parked at a meter too long, and traffic violations are all subject to fines. At home and in school fines can be applied in the form of detentions, extra work and even money. One mother with four children had a nightmare each time she took them shopping. "I want this," and "Buy me that." You know the routine. Invariably Mom would wind up spending a small fortune on food for bribes just to shut the kids up, which only reinforced them to beg and holler next time.

Roger suggested she begin the next shopping trip by announcing, "Today we're going shopping. I'm going to give each of you enough money to buy one ice cream cone" (she had been spending more than that, anyway). "If you act up, argue or fight, I'll fine you five cents for each time. You'll have to pay me right then out of your ice cream money" (she kept the two youngest kids' money to avoid their losing it). "When we get to the ice cream parlor at the end of our shopping" (arranged that way on purpose) "you can buy anything you want with your money or you can save it for another time."

The logical consequence at the end of their shopping was that those who had behaved could still afford an ice cream cone and those who had acted up went without. Her kids improved dramatically in just one trip using this consequence. (Some kids need more than one time.) Mom began to enjoy shopping for the first time in years. Eventually the kids acted right, without needing the ice cream money because good behavior became a habit.

The "Friend" and "Provider" parenting style have the most problem setting and holding to the consequences. It comes most natural to the "Nurturer" style. The "Boss" style sees it as a waste of time. The children should obey because the "Boss" has spoken, period.

Time-out

Time-out is a little like "go stand in the corner" for a specified amount of time. However, there's much more to it than that. Time-out is removing your child from the present situation and giving him some time to think. God used the wilderness as a perfect time-out place for His children when they misbehaved. The desert is a great place to think—there's little else to do for forty years.

For a preschool child three minutes for the first time-out of the day is appropriate, and for a school-aged child five minutes is about right. If your child needs a second time-out later that day for the same behavior, try adding additional time. Roger recommends you start at the beginning for a different misbehavior and always start each day with a clean slate.

An ideal time-out corner has no windows to look out and nothing handy to play with. Preferably it's a boring spot away from the main activity in your house. You should be able to see your child at all times, but he must face away from you into the wall or a corner. If you don't have any corners handy, you might tell your child to sit on the edge of the bathtub or stand in a utility room so long as the door remains open and you can see him easily. Friends, brothers and sisters aren't allowed to talk to a child in time-out or else they get a time-out of their own.

Getting Started Right

For safety's sake and to avoid panic, never put a child in a small confined place like a closet and never close the door of the room when a child is in time-out. When you first begin using time-out, periodically check on your child to see how he's doing. Avoid using time-out for children who are prone to daydream, since time-out will be a rewarding place to daydream more. Depressed children will only become more depressed in time-out, so try something different, perhaps negative practice (more on that later).

Time-out is suitable for misbehavior like refusing to cooperate, deliberately moving slowly (stalling for time), or doing something other than you told your child to do like continuing to watch TV after you said, "Turn it off." When Lane needed time-out, Kathy or Roger would say, "All right, Lane, that's time-out because you kept on —. Go to the time-out corner and stay there until the timer goes off." Then we set the timer on our kitchen stove.

If you need to buy a timer, there are small digital models that can be easily programmed for 1-100 minutes and are magnetized to stay on your refrigerator. Punch in the time you want, like a calculator, press "start," and go about your business.

If your child starts to yell or ask, "How much longer?" answer, "Each time you yell or leave the corner I'll add one more minute to your time. Stay there quietly until the timer goes off." If he continues to complain keep adding extra minutes up to a maximum of ten beyond the original time. This works for most kids, but if yours tests you beyond the extra ten minutes you'll need to shift gears and try something different.

Time-out for Small Children

Small children can be put in time-out by using a high chair with the seat and crotch belts safely fastened so your child can't climb or slip out. Adjust the tray snugly up so your child is better restrained and can't loosen the safety belts. Place the high chair far enough away from the wall so he can't push himself over backwards with his feet and can't reach or grab anything. It will work best if your child can't see or hear you easily. The Allens started putting Lane in time-out when he was fourteen months old when he seemed to take great delight in filling his little hands with food and smearing the stuff all over his high chair. Time-out worked! He stopped!

Some parents use a playpen for time-out. Just be sure there are no toys to play with and that the mesh is small enough to keep buttons and snaps on your child's clothing from getting caught. At first most small children will cry and scream like a stuck pig when placed in time-out. It usually takes them five to ten times in time-out before they'll settle down and get quiet quickly. It takes that long for them to learn that the time-out period is short and that when the timer goes off they'll be able to return to their play. It's important for you to do your part by letting a child out of time-out as soon as the timer goes off.

Children who are too old for a high chair or playpen can be told to sit in a small chair, which will reduce the temptation for them to walk off. By age three or four most children will cooperate by sitting in the chair. By age eight most can stand facing the wall.

Occasionally a small child will not leave time-out even when the timer has sounded and his parents have given permission to leave. The child's embarrassment and shame keep him there, and he may be trying to put a little guilt on you for putting him in time-out. If this happens just say, "You are welcome to leave time-out as soon as you decide, but if you want to stay, that's up to you. When you feel like getting out of time-out and having fun again, you may." Then the parent should leave the room to avoid giving the child negative attention for having stayed in time-out too long.

The Place for Time-out

Most children's rooms are so full of toys, electronic gear and books that sending a child to his room is not the place for time-out. Besides, do you want to associate the place where your child sleeps and plays with punishment?

Some parents will send their child out of a room, "Until you can behave." When that happens the child usually walks halfway down the hall, realizes he's about to miss out on the best part of the TV show, and suddenly decides to be good. This is actually a form of manipulation because the child simply cooperates with time-out until he's ready to switch it off on his own terms. It doesn't work that way in real life. In real life, once the blinking red lights appear in the rearview mirror, you're going to get a ticket. It doesn't matter how nice you are between the time you got the ticket and when you pay it, the fine is still the same. And if you get too sassy with the officer giving you the ticket, something else may be added to it as well.

Giving Instructions Once

Usually one warning is appropriate for each new problem, sometimes none if the child clearly knows his actions are off limits. Once the warning has been issued, be ready to follow through with an appropriate consequence. After all, each traffic signal has one caution light, but when the signal turns red, it's time to stop.

Many parents will count from one to three before following through with some consequence. Roger saw a funny example of this with some friends. They had two children, ages two and four. Betty, the four year old, was playing in the backyard. Dad came out and said, "Betty, it's time for supper." Betty kept right on playing, acting as if she hadn't heard, even though it was obvious she had. "Betty," he said, "come in right now!" You know the routine. Betty went right on playing and jumping around, dah-te-dah-te-day. "Betty! That's ONE!" dah-te-dah-te-dah. "That's TWO!" Same song and dance from Betty. "That's TWO AND ONE-HALF. . ., TWO AND THREE-FOURTHS. . . , TWO AND SEVEN-EIGHTHS! ALL RIGHT! THAT DOES IT. DO I HAVE TO GET MY BELT?" It wasn't until Dad's voice got loud enough and his look stern enough that Betty decided she had waited as long as she dared. Then she came in. Her only punishment was Dad's loud voice.

Actually, I was impressed. After all, here was this four year old who ordinarily wouldn't learn fractions until the third grade, and already her father was teaching them to her. Imagine that! He actually said, "Two and seven-eighths!" Betty knew Dad well enough to stall until his breaking point was almost reached. I wonder what would have happened if Dad simply had told her once that supper was ready and then had gone back inside to eat.

Time-out is used most by the "Nurturer"-style parent. The "Provider" parent has the most problem using time-out because it takes planning and effort.

Negative Practice

Negative practice combines time-out with children practicing the very action you want them to stop, over and over for three to five minutes. It works because most children soon get tired of misbehaviors they are told they have to do. Remember, the goal is to help the child. For example, "Because you kept jumping on the bed after I told you to stop, go over to the time-out corner and jump up and down until the timer goes off." As with regular time-out, walk away as soon as you set the timer or else your child will try to talk you out of the punishment or will ask you endless questions to diminish the boredom. Be sure the timer is well out of his reach, preferably in another room, where he can still hear it go off. Periodically check to be sure your child is cooperating with your instructions.

Negative practice makes misbehaviors boomerang and then stop due to saturation. Once we become saturated with an activity, most of us soon tire of it. Many of the negative things kids do to get attention are appealing because they know it's against the rules. Giving children "permission" to repeat those things in a time-out corner for three to five minutes soon spoils the taboo appeal.

If you have a stubborn child who likes to test your resolve, he might say, "I'll stay in the corner, but you can't make me jump up and down." You might say, "Of course not, and I wouldn't think of trying to make you, but for every minute you stall me by not jumping, you're going to lose two minutes from your next TV show or play activity, and you have lost five minutes just now for stalling. As soon as you decide to start jumping up and down, tell me so I'll know when to stop counting your penalty time." Then walk out of the room. If your child remains in time-out until the timer goes off, but never begins to jump, no problem. It'll just catch up with him later when he wants to start watching TV or play outside. Simply say, "Ordinarily that would be fine with me, but remember earlier when I told you to jump up and down and you refused to do it? That was thirty minutes ago and two times thirty is sixty minutes or one hour. That's how long you're going to have to wait before watching TV or going outside to play. If bedtime comes before you use up the time you'll just have to finish the remaining penalty tomorrow."

Punishment

Spanking

Punishment, in the form of pain, works best with young children, usually before they reach the third or fourth grade. Even then, spanking is an "iffy" proposition. Many times parents spank more out of their own frustration than because it works. To be most effective, spanking should be used as a reaction to a major problem. If we aren't careful, using spanking for minor problems is like using a chain saw to build a picture frame. It may work, but you'll probably do more than you wanted to; frequently after you've finished, nothing fits like you intended it to. It doesn't make much sense to spank for minor problems when we can probably help children act better with more appropriate kinds of discipline.

We think it's best to reserve spanking for open defiance and rebellious behavior in children roughly two to ten years of age. Defiance and rebellion are deliberate challenges to a parent's authority so it's time to step in and take prompt action. Also you might use spanking with very small children, about two to four years old who violate safety rules like running into the street or sticking things into electrical outlets. When a child is too young to reason with or understand other kinds of punishment, you don't want to "discuss" unsafe behavior, you just want it to stop.

Spanking tends to stop misbehavior but not teach the correct behavior. This reality points up its limitation in teaching our children.

Spanking Older Kids

After children reach the third or fourth grade, spanking becomes largely ineffective because of the increased padding in most children's rear ends. If you decide to spank, before you begin decide whether to use one, two or three swats. Tell your child, "I'm going to give you (1, 2, 3) swats," and then get it over with.

Roger knows some parents who made their son pull his jeans down when they spanked him in order to cause more pain. That seems downright mean to us and probably resulted in the boy feeling antagonistic toward his parents. In the same way, it's unwise to keep spanking until your child starts to scream and cry. Some children, out of spite or pride or hurt, will do anything to avoid crying. And if you keep spanking until they cry you may risk child abuse.

Paddling

Frankly, neither of us cares for paddles. We feel a child will likely see them for what they are, weapons of punishment. We don't think parents need to be in the business of using weapons. Using your hand is one thing, but using a belt or paddle because it hurts more seems unreasonable to us. Remember, the purpose of spanking is to discipline the child, not relieve the frustration of the parent. Doesn't that make sense?

Punishment is anything that is unpleasant to a child that comes as a result of that child's actions. Physical pain, such as spanking, may not be all that unpleasant. Think back to when you were a kid. What one of us by the fifth grade wouldn't have preferred a quick spanking than being grounded for an entire week? The sting of a spanking rarely lasts for more than fifteen minutes, but take away an allowance, the telephone or ground a child for a weekend and the punishment seems like forever.

Potential Problems with Punishment

Punishment often fails to teach desirable actions; it only suppresses an action. But if a child is running into the street, then all you want to do is to stop that action, so punishment is appropriate. However, punishment does have some built-in problems. This is especially true when the child doubts whether he is loved. Paul admonishes, "Fathers, do not embitter your children, or they will become discouraged" (Colossians 3:21). Embitterment has three aspects:

Resentment. Punishment can result in resentment by both child and parent. If the punishment you administer doesn't relate to the behavior that took place, you run the risk of the child becoming resentful. For example, spanking a child for marking on a wall has nothing to do with that behavior. Or spanking one child for hitting another child makes little sense when the lesson you want the child to learn is to avoid hitting. When the punishment doesn't make sense, resentment is born.

Backlash. One of the problems with strong punishment, especially spanking, is its potential to backfire on us, especially if we have a so-called strong-willed child. Parents learn early that spanking might stop behavior temporarily, but later their child might do it again and again just to defy us. So be careful out there!

Overkill/Child Abuse. All too often child abuse begins as

punishment that gets out of hand. I've seen so many good parents who have expressed their personal pain and horror at how easy it was for spanking to get out of hand. A parent tends to become desensitized to spanking, and so does the child. Gradually, like a person who develops resistance to a particular kind of medication through repeated use, it takes more and more to do the job. That's why it's especially important that, if you choose to spank, you decide ahead of time to use only one to three swats to avoid the punishment getting out of hand. Making this simple decision will provide immediate help.

Defeatism. Finally, if you need further reason to consider using other forms of discipline than punishment, think about this: Chris is always getting punished, excessively punished. He used to rebel and fight. Now, he is discouraged and depressed. He feels that nothing he does is worthwhile and that he gets punished no matter what he does. Chris has now given up on everything—"Why try?" Children who stop trying soon feel hopeless and helpless. They feel unloved and worthless and lectures will never convince them otherwise. Cutting off children's initiative through defeatism is like cutting off their emotional air. It's a cruel form of suffocation because while the child's heart keeps beating his spirit dies bit by bit.

Remember, the main thing children learn from punishment is what not to do, not what to do. It takes common sense and an atmosphere of love to make it work right.

Character Testing

In his last sermon series Moses revealed how God led, tested and humbled His children to see what was in their hearts. It seems to us that it would be appropriate for parents to do the same. This part of parenting is beyond the bounds of a "Provider" style parent. But it is this type of involvement that makes the "Nurturer" style so effective.

We believe parents should always have the ultimate say, but at times all kids need enough rope to hang themselves, so to speak. Remember, God led His children of Israel into the desert, gave them instructions and rules. He tested them to see what was in their heart—to see how mature they were. Parents have to test too.

Key to Success

A little discipline often works better than a lot. That's why no TV for five minutes is often worse than no TV for the evening. Restrict a child from TV for the evening and he'll simply find something else to do for fun. Make him miss five minutes while standing in time-out, and he's dying to get back to see what he's missing. Forget grounding for a month or longer because it will punish the whole family as much as the child. A little discipline carefully designed is better than a lot.

If defiance persists, family counseling is recommended. Spanking small children, up to the third or fourth grade, may break the will enough to start fresh. For older children, even through teenage years, it may be necessary to strip their rooms of nonessentials, leaving them with only the basics. Then anything they want back they'd have to earn back. Make a list of the "prices" of things and what it would take to get them back in terms of hours of study, improved grades, work around the house, and so on. Don't make it unreasonable or hopeless to obtain, but sufficiently serious to show that you mean business.

This worked well with one especially sullen and sassy teenager. It took one week for her to realize her parents were no longer going to put up with her disobedience. Some children are almost daring their parents to lay down the law. When that happens, you'll be doing your kids a favor if you do. When the kids are honest, they'll tell you they want to be disciplined.

Parents should remember: If you want children to learn responsibility, you'll have to give them some. If you want children to learn accountability, you'll have to hold them accountable. Some of the best lessons children learn throughout life are those that hurt. Having to pay the price when young may well keep children from bigger problems later.

Considering the Options

We've now overviewed four methods of common sense discipline. Each of these methods can be adapted to each child and any situation.

The rest of this book will show you how these methods work in actual practice at each age level. Remember to demonstrate your love and support, emphasize the positive, and listen carefully to your child's conversations. Mention the things you appreciate and notice what they do well: "I really appreciate the pleasant way you've been acting this morning. It's fun to be with you." Positive statement from you will help all the discipline methods work better.

Don't forget the goal: common sense discipline will help you raise resourceful children who have learned how to be responsible adults.

CHAPTER 5
Guiding Their First Steps
—12-30 Months

OF ALL THE LESSONS YOU WANT YOUR child to learn, which is most important during the early years? Obeying, walking, talking, or sharing? What's the most important thing you want to teach your child during this period?

When Julie and Joy were this age, more than anything else Ron wanted them to learn about love. Love is, without a doubt, the most important lesson anyone learns in life and the early years are critical to the foundation of love.

The Nature of Love

Babies provide us with on-the-job love experience. While we are busy teaching them about love, they are innocently teaching us too. Real love is doing something for someone else that you don't have to do, that you may not even want to do, but that you choose to do because you have the other person's best interest at heart. Jesus' sacrifice on the cross is the ultimate example of unconditional love. It was His choice.

Love is our choice even if it means changing dirty diapers, changing plans or changing our mind.

Since 1977 when Ron began using this example, only one adult has said she actually enjoyed changing dirty diapers, and she may have been a bit disturbed. The fact of the matter is that changing dirty diapers is an unpleasant business, at least for the person doing the changing. Ron did find that he enjoyed getting up at 3:00 A.M. to comfort his frightened daughter because he loved the feeling he got when she clung to him for protection and security.

But changing dirty diapers? It's a dirty, stinking job, that's for sure. We do it because we love. We do it even when we don't feel like it—because we love.

Common Sense Discipline Chart 2

Chart 2 indicates the need for parents to make the major decisions for infants—that's common sense! There is, howev-

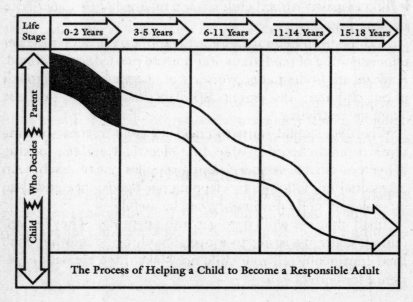

| Life Stage | 0-2 Years | 3-5 Years | 6-11 Years | 11-14 Years | 15-18 Years |

The Process of Helping a Child to Become a Responsible Adult er, a need for little babies to be able to pick and choose very early in life. It's great practice for the big decisions later on.

First Six Months

During the first six months of life, the most important discipline your child needs is your love, attention and protection. Roger's pediatrician told them shortly after Lane was born that for the first six months, "You can't spoil him by giving too much attention." That's proven to be absolutely sound advice. During this time, talking, playing, and protecting are the most important things to do.

A child's life prior to this century was somewhat bleak. Even as late as the 19th Century it was the assumed job of the parent to be harsh, firm, and restrictive. Only recently have we realized that children need comfort and nurture, help and encouragement. Dr. Lloyd deMause, an American psychohistorian and editor of *History of Childhood Quarterly*, has found that not only do children need help in growing up, but that feeling empathy toward children is a relatively new experience in American history.

God has been helping us for generations to develop a deeper understanding of tenderness and nurture needed in childhood. And we are finding effective ways of encouraging the growth of our children. But parents of infants must also at times be "lovingly restrictive."

When your child starts to crawl it's time to start showing some common sense in shielding electrical outlets, locking dangerous chemicals and cleaning supplies out of reach. An occasional no, followed by clapping our hands once and then moving your child if necessary, can be useful.

Small children will try to get into anything. They're curious. Usually it's easier to move something to another shelf than continually tell your child no. Make this a pleasant experience for both of you.

Six to Thirty Months

These first few years are full of exciting changes in you and your child. Have you thought about how you change during these months? The baby makes dramatic changes. You'll witness some important changes in your baby including: walking (12-18 months), talking (12-24 months), toilet training (18-30 months)and temper tantrums (18-30 months). Let's start with the fun part.

Walking

Some children crawl a long time before they start walking; some just seem to get up one day and walk on their own. Walking is probably learned as a combination of instinct and imitation. For months your baby has noticed all of the fun things you keep up high and how fun it is to ride while you walk. When the time is right he'll try walking on his own.

When Your Child Is Hurt

Learning to walk is reinforced by praise and encouragement. It's also accompanied by falls and bumps. The way parents respond to these accidents will teach children a great deal about pain.

For most young children, pain is largely psychological. That's not to say children don't get hurt physically; they do. But a great deal of their pain can be avoided if parents respond appropriately to accidents. It's important for parents to help children minimize the effects of pain because so many bumps are inevitable during this period, and unnecessary attention for pain will teach children to become whiners and cry babies. Adult hypochondriacs don't get that way by accident.

Next time you're around a toddler and his parents, watch what happens when the toddler falls. Usually the child will immediately look to Mom and Dad for a reaction. If they say in alarm, "Oh, my poor darling, are you all right?" you can expect Junior to get scared and start crying. Then Mom or Dad will pick him up and sympathize with him, which only reinforces Junior's decision to get scared and cry.

Asking a child, "Are you hurt?" guarantees that he will think about pain. Our looks of alarm and concern will trigger Junior to get scared and cry, if for no other reason than our scared facial expressions.

When a child stumbles and falls parents might try saying, "OK?" with a questioning but reassuring expression. Instead of showing shock and alarm, a matter-of-fact attitude says, "It's all right to have bumps and falls." If the child continues to stay on the floor, say, "Need a hand?" instead of, "Here, let me help you up," which would suggest he probably can't handle this problem.

Rather than give too much attention to pain, here are three reassuring statements to say to your child:

1. "I know it hurts" acknowledges the pain and shows that you understand what your child is experiencing.

2. "It will get better" offers reassurance that the pain doesn't last forever.

3. "Tell me when you feel better" distracts your child from the pain and has a positive, self-fulfilling prophetic effect.

Using these three statements with Lane brought some pleasant results. One is that he has a very high tolerance to pain. He rarely cries in response to a bump or sickness, but when he does, we know that he's genuinely in pain. A lighter note occurred once when some friends were visiting, and their children were playing with Lane in his room. In his excitement, Lane fell and bruised his knee. In obvious pain, he came limping to me for comfort. After Roger used the three love statements, Lane got up, still hurting but eager to return to his friends, and said, "I feel better now, Daddy. I feel better." And, he limped back into action.

Baby-Proofing Your House

Most parents automatically "baby-proof" their houses by removing glass objects and padding sharp corners where possible. While it's a good idea to remove all the potentially dangerous objects infants may be attracted to, have you replaced those things with safe substitutes for your child to play with? Here's how the Allens did it.

In our living room there are two cabinets in the bottom of a bookcase. Lane could easily crawl into the cabinets and reach the first shelf above the cabinets. We could see that it was going to be trouble, trouble, trouble keeping him away from valuable objects there, so we decided to store some of Lane's favorite toys here. So we reserved the two cabinets and the first shelf for his friends and him.

When our friends came over with their children we'd open the cabinets and tell the kids, "Here are some things for you to play with," and the kids would make a bee-line for them. Because the toys were in easy reach, all the children tended to stay in the immediate area around the cabinets. Occasionally a child would climb into the cabinets and close the doors, but that was all part of their fun. Having only toys in the cabinets and shelf made clean-up easy, too. We'd toss the toys into the cabinets and shut the doors. The most appealing toys went on the first shelf in plain view. When the kids came over again they'd go straight for the cabinets and take out the toys and begin playing. At first their parents would scold them for their assertiveness and for "Not asking first," but we'd reassure the parents, "It's okay; they know that's what the toys are there for."

Christmas Trees

Your child's first or second Christmas tree can be a special memory, or it can be a real headache depending on how you arrange things. Some parents unnecessarily spend time spanking a child's hands for touching the ornaments. That seems a bit naive and unrealistic because the ornaments are pretty to look at and fascinating to touch. Say no in such a situation and you set yourself for defiance.

One rather eccentric couple decided to suspend their

Christmas tree from the ceiling so that it was off the floor, above their toddler's reach. That way everyone could enjoy it without having to fuss at the child. Granted, it did look a bit unusual, but it was safe and solved the problem of their child reaching for the ornaments or trying to pull the tree over. Other parents have found it useful to put their Christmas tree inside a playpen to provide an instant security fence, keeping children away from the tree.

When Lane was very small, Kathy and Roger bought a little tree and placed it on top of a table, out of his reach. It's important for parents to recognize the obvious. Little children ages one to two are fascinated by Christmas trees and will naturally gravitate towards one. Instead of trying to change the child's natural and almost impossible-to-control curiosity towards a tree, it's easier to change our plans, since the tree will be up for only a few weeks. At most you'll probably have to deal with this particular problem once or twice. Remember to use caution when other small children come over after yours are bigger and your tree is out.

Talking

About the same time children are learning to walk they begin talking. As with walking, they'll make lots of mistakes while learning to talk. Be patient and allow them room for trial and error. When a child mispronounces a word, either say nothing or answer by using the word correctly. Stuttering frequently begins from an over-emphasis on correct speech. If you're patient, there's less chance that stuttering problems will develop.

If your child starts to stutter, be patient, avoiding looking directly at your child because that seems to heighten the tension and anxiety. If your child keeps balking, say, "When you think of the answer later, will you tell me?"

When children are learning to speak they will often point and whine for attention when they already know the word they want to use, such as "milk." When you see your child begin to do this and realize she is pointing rather than speaking, act as if you don't understand and say, "I'm not sure what you want but I'm sure you do. Say the right word, please." Of course your child will get frustrated and may have a minor fit at first, but if you're patient, most children will soon start saying the right word again.

Fussing

Fussing is a problem for all children at some time. When children are tired, worn out and ready for a nap, fussing sometimes keeps them awake. (Remember, little ones hate to give in to a nap.) Fussing can become chronic, however; in that case, it needs to be nipped in the bud before it becomes a habit. Parents could tune out their children's complaints, forcing one of two general reactions: (1) child feeling ignored and unloved or (2) child increasing volume and sometimes increasing frequency.

Either way, the parent ends up the loser. When children fuss, tell them, "That's fussing and you must stop or else you can go to the time-out corner and 'fuss-fuss-fuss' until the timer goes off." If your child continues to fuss, then allow him the opportunity to fuss in the corner.

Toilet Training

A typical time to begin thinking about toilet training is about 18-30 months of age. No doubt you'll hear lots of advice from well-meaning friends and relatives who want to impose their advice on you. Avoid letting them do so, because toilet training is up to your child and you. Here are some major considerations:

First, your child must be old enough and strong enough to sit unsupported on a child's potty or commode. If he can't sit unsupported, then he's definitely not ready. If he's too scared to sit on the commode, then don't force the issue and try again in a few weeks.

Second, your child will need to have an incentive to want to begin toilet training, such as a desire to stop wearing diapers, or becoming a "big boy/girl" like Johnny or Christi. One advantage of enrolling a child in a Sunday School or Mother's Day Out program is the opportunity to see other children using a toilet and wanting to be able to do what they can do.

Third, parents must be willing to stop whatever they are doing and spend the time necessary to go to the toilet with their child when the need is expressed. This will mean interrupting conversations, meals, and shopping trips. Unless you and your child are ready for these three considerations then don't even attempt toilet training.

During this training period children frequently become fascinated with public restrooms. They'll say they need to go to the bathroom; once there, they will look around and then ask to leave. You may think your child has developed some strange preoccupations with public restrooms, since every time you sit down to a meal in a restaurant your child has to "go potty." Stay calm; "this too shall pass." Once children learn the location and arrangement of public restrooms, their fascination tends to diminish. It's simply a way children learn about their world, and it's an important part of their education. After all, one of their fears as they begin toilet training is that they'll have an accident, so going to the restroom on a dry run is like practicing for a fire drill. It's a good preventative step for your child and you, so cooperate like a good sport.

If Your Child Has an Accident

First, never, never shame a child for having an accident. He's not a "bad boy" for a slip up, so don't say it. We adults have accidents of one sort or another, and no one calls us "bad grown-ups" when we make mistakes. Second, shaming a child because of any accidental behavior whether it be toilet training, stuttering or being clumsy tends to add to the anxiety and may make your child more likely to have another accident the next time. In fact, insurance actuaries point out that just having an accident tends to set us up to be more likely to have another soon.

When your child wets or soils himself, simply clean up the mess with as little fuss as possible. Reassure the child with, "No big deal, I used to have accidents when I was your age, too." Then go about business as usual. If you reassure children and minimize the effects of accidents, they'll reward you with more self-confident behavior and fewer accidents.

Using a Star Chart

The following is a Star Chart and a set of rules that can be used to help toilet trained your child. Began using the system generally around thirty months of age. Tape a chart to the refrigerator at his eye level and purchased stars at a variety store. As your child earns stars he gets to stick them on the chart. Completed charts containing two rows of five stars each could be used for a trip to McDonald's or some other special treat. After your child is trained, continue to use the chart for several months and then gradually phase them out.

Star Chart

Rules: "You will get one star for urinating and two stars for a bowel movement. If you have a dry diaper and pants when you wake up you will get two more stars. When you have stars in all the boxes in both rows, you can go to McDonald's (or some similar treat). If you go to bed wearing training pants but wake up wet in the morning, you'll have to wear diapers to help stay dry that night. If you wake up with a dry diaper the next morning, you can try training pants again."

Note: Instead of telling all the rules at once, repeat portions of them, when appropriate, to encourage him each time he earns another star. At first each chart should contain two rows of five boxes each, for a total of ten. Each time your child has a successful trip to the bathroom or a dry night, he

Star Chart

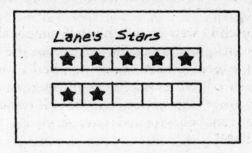

earns one to three stars which are placed in one box. Soon he will be able to fill several boxes with stars each day. As your child becomes more proficient and completed charts quickly, increase the number of boxes from ten to twelve, then to fourteen.

The Temporary Twos

Most of you have already heard about the Terrible Twos—that period from about eighteen months of age to around three years. Let me tell you about Robin.

Robin's father, Ralph, is still in shock. This cute little two year old has made an unforgettable impression on everyone who knows her. Her trail of disasters began with the toilet. Alice the cat got dunked, drowned and flushed. A few days later Robin decided to give teddy bear a bath: she set him on top of the heating element in the dishwasher. The bear came out a crispy critter.

Robin then attacked the refrigerator. She stuck some magnetic letters in the vents just before the family took a weekend trip, causing the motor to burn out.

Next day Robin's mother left her asleep in her car seat while she went in the post office to mail a letter. When she came out she discovered Robin driving the car straight into a tree.

A week later Robin's mom and dad parked their car halfway in the garage after a shopping trip because they were planning to unload groceries. Robin was strapped in the car seat, and her mother had the keys. While the parents were in the kitchen they heard loud noises from the garage. When they got outside they found the automatic garage door bouncing up and down on the hood of the car with you know who inside pushing the button. Within just a few weeks Robin's damages cost $2,296.37. She is a prime example of the Terrible Twos.

The good news is that this is a time-limited phase and usually disappears around a child's third birthday. Robin's parents celebrated her third birthday in style.

Tantrums

One of the major symptoms of the Terrible Twos is the tantrums that children throw at any and all places, especially in grocery stores and when we have company. Usually the tantrum is a result of the child's not getting his way. Tantrums usually get a child a lot of negative attention. Tantrums can be compared to the comedy routines of Bob Hope, Bill Cosby, and Carol Burnett. All three are comedians, with distinctly different kinds of humor, but they all have one thing in common: When the audience walks out, the clown stops the act. And that's what a tantrum is, an act on your child's part to pressure you to give in. The best way to respond when your child tries to bluff you is to call the bluff firmly and quickly.

If the tantrum takes place while you have company present, tell your child, "I have a feeling you're acting up on purpose in front of my guest, so go to your time-out corner for three minutes. If you keep up the fit you will have to practice it the entire time-out time." Tell your guest, "I'm sorry about that, but we're having to stop this routine in order to make things better."

Public Demonstrations

In the supermarket a man was pushing a grocery cart that

contained a screaming, yelling, bellowing two year old. The gentleman kept repeating such admonitions as "Don't get excited, Albert," "Don't scream, Albert," "Don't yell, Albert."

A woman standing next to him said, "You certainly are to be commended for trying to soothe your son, Albert."

The man looked at her and said soberly, "Lady, *I'm* Albert!"

Unfortunately, many parents feel years of empty threats and hours of yelling are a more humane way of dealing with the tantrum. We're convinced just the opposite is true.

When you take children into a public place remember the reality of the child's age and the setting. Most children under thirty months of age just aren't ready to sit through a long meal. To avoid frustration, either go to a fast-food restaurant or get a baby sitter when you want to go out for a big meal.

Where Do They Learn That?

Ah, those two year olds. Just about the time you think you've conquered the temporary twos they surprise you with their insight into human emotions. Roger tells of a wonderful little dialogue between him and Lane. Lane was barely two years old.

We were eating dinner when Lane, still upset at being disciplined, looked me straight in the eye and said, "I'll never speak to you again!" Where did those words come from? He had only been speaking in sentences for a few months. I guess sentences like that are handed down, generation to generation, on the playgrounds, in the church nurseries and in day-care centers across America. They come to kids mysteriously, like the rules to "Hide-and-Seek."

A few weeks after that episode Lane threatened to "run away."

"I'd hate to see you do that, Son. What about your toys?"

"Huh? What do you mean?"

"Well, if you're going to leave here, you won't be able to take all your toys with you, and we won't need them. So do you want me to give them to one of your friends?"

He thought about that for a few minutes and decided, "I think I'll stay. Can I have a drink?"

These surprising little moments are what help parents and kids survive the temporary twos—with joy!

Typical Childhood Fears

Toddlers naturally develop some common fears. They may end up fearing a thing that to us seems silly, but to them it's terrifying. They fear things like:

Their parents being lost forever when they are out of sight in the other room.

The vacuum cleaner running over them.

The shampoo putting their eyes out.

Slipping down the bathtub drain or disappearing down the toilet.

The "monsters" in the closet, under the bed or in the dark.

The pain of getting part of their body cut off and thrown away—their hair.

A dog biting them.

Accept the fears as real; remove the child from the fearful situation and talk about the situation. Help him to go back and confront his fears.

Fear of Strangers

Many children develop a strong "stranger anxiety." They hide, cry and sometimes scream when they are around people they don't know. Instead of saying, "There's nothing to be afraid of," briefly explain to your child what's going on: "That's the man who delivers the mail to us. Let's go see what he brought."

Fear of Separation

While the fear of strangers typically occurs when a child is in a parent's presence, fear of separation is a time of uneasiness that takes place when a child discovers he's been left alone by Mom or Dad. Typically this begins about eighteen months of age and decreases between two and three years. When separation anxiety takes place at home, your child may go from room to room looking for you. It's especially upsetting to parents when they leave their child with a trusted babysitter who previously cared for the child successfully, but now Junior has suddenly started to cry and panic.

The best way to handle separation anxiety is to explain to the baby sitter what's going on. Then tell your child Mommy will be back, "after you've had dinner," or "after you've gone to bed but before you wake up in the morning." (Give your child something of yours to keep for you while you're gone. This helps assure the child that you'll come back.) Then leave, despite the cries of panic. You almost have to handle this "cold turkey" because all the reassurance in the world will only make your child more fearful and clinging and leaves you feeling guilty. Besides, sooner or later your child will have to accept other adults in charge. The sooner he gets adjusted to separating from his parents, the better.

Baby Sitters

Leaving your child with a sitter for the first time is usually tougher on you than on your child. Naturally he's going to cry, and you're going to feel like you're abandoning your child. The concerned parents are fearful of what might happen. The following "How to Prepare the Baby Sitter" list can be a great comfort to the parents as well as to the sitter.

How to Prepare the Baby Sitter

Tour the house to locate telephones, exits, first aid supplies, flashlight, play areas.

Discuss food habits, bedtime, favorite activities, special appliances, TV rules, medicines, allergies, other health problems.

Confirm expected time of return.

Make a telephone number list, including where you will be,

a neighbor's number, emergency numbers.

Make arrangements for the fee you will pay.

Point out the pad for telephone messages and return numbers.

Demonstrate any unusual locks on doors and inform the sitter of your desire for the doors to be locked while you're gone.

Suggest sitter privileges, such as TV, food, visitors, telephone calls.

Write any "special instructions" down so there will be no misunderstanding.

Leaving Baby Overnight

How early is too early to leave a baby with someone while you're gone overnight? That depends on your situation. One physician recommends to new parents that when their newborn is three months old they make arrangements for the baby to be kept by grandparents or trusted friends while they go away for a few days for a second honeymoon. I think that's excellent advice, both for the baby and the parents.

For whatever reason, if you have a need to get away from your children for a few days, do it. Find some friends or relatives and form a child-care co-op. You will sit for their children, and they can take care of yours. If you're not sure how they'll respond to such a deal, offer to take care of their kids first. In essence, you're offering to "pay in advance," so it's easier to make the suggestion.

Now I Have Some Options

The first thirty months are times when every parent will feel stressed and a little trapped. Babies take a lot of time and energy, but with common sense discipline you always have options. Knowing you have options helps you get past the rough spots and even the temporary terrible two's.

Knowing what to say and do in specific situations can help you concentrate on enjoying your kids. When parenting is an enjoyable experience, you will naturally be more loving and tolerant. Remember, this book is designed to help, not judge. Nobody is perfect, so hang in there, you're doing fine.

CHAPTER 6
Exploring the World with Limits

3-5 Years

SHORTLY AFTER TURNING FIVE, one little boy interrupted a disagreement with his father by yelling, "I want to be adopted!"

The father responded, "Listen, maybe you can't stand it here and maybe you don't like me very much. I understand, because sometimes I don't like me either. But even with the problem we're having right now, I still love you, and I always will. You're my boy, and I'm proud of you. There's just no way I'm ever going to allow you to be adopted. That's final, so we might as well look for some ways to get along with each other and start having some fun again."

"Do you want to play checkers?" the boy asked. "That's fun!"

The preschool years are filled with "little surprises."

Chart 3 pictures a little more freedom of choice for the preschooler within the fences of the parent's decisions. Young

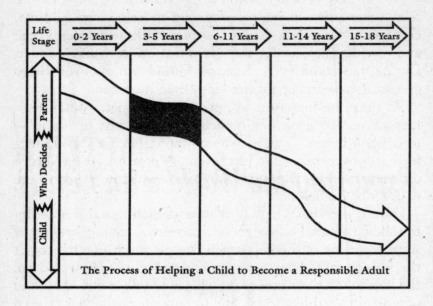

Life Stage	0-2 Years	3-5 Years	6-11 Years	11-14 Years	15-18 Years

The Process of Helping a Child to Become a Responsible Adult

children from three to five years old are wondering wanderers. They love to explore, touch, watch, and taste almost anything. Their daily adventures are fun to watch, and conversation is a joy. Give them lots of choices—choices of colors, sizes, shapes, foods, activities, etc. But, remember, you still call the shots. You're the one who's in charge. You see the future; they only see today.

Conversations of Wonder

The years from three to five are fascinating for parents. Simple conversations become trips into fantasyland. Learning to use words to tell about what's happening inside us is stimulating to most youngsters. At times it's entertaining to listen to the three to five year old tell about life from his perspective.

Not all talk is designed to be an exchange of information. Sometimes you will use conversation to help your child discover something new. These discovery talks will require time and a willingness to let the conversation flow and wander. During these talks both parent and child will discover things and set themselves up for similar talks in the future.

At times we just want to hear about feelings. When feelings are negative, our first tendency will be to try to "fix it"— to make it better. The most important thing we can do in a feeling conversation is to just listen. A preschooler has lots of different feelings. He just doesn't have as many words to use to describe his feelings.

During the 1950s, Art Linkletter demonstrated the ability to talk with preschoolers about discoveries, feelings and other surprises. One of the keys to his success was his ability to get the kids to talk about their pretend thoughts. He would ask the kids to tell their innermost wishes, to talk about what kind of animal they'd like to be, and to announce what ages they'd prefer to be and why. You never knew when one of those talks would make your day.

Art Linkletter tells the story of a little boy who listened attentively to his Sunday school teacher tell about a familiar Bible passage. She read, "From dust thou art and to dust thou shalt return." The little boy's mind captured that phrase, and as soon as he got home, he looked under his bed and ran to his mother.

"Mom, is it true that God makes people out of dust?"

"Yes," Mom said.

"Mom, is it true that we're dust after we're dead?"

"Yes, why?"

"Well, go look under my bed, quick! Somebody's either coming or going!"

The three to five year old will sometimes mix up the facts.

For instance, kids have rewritten the lyrics of some famous songs. Have you heard these new song lyrics?

"I'm going to Alabama with a Band-Aid on my knee."

"Gladly, the cross-eyed bear."

"Stand beside her, and guide her, with the light through the night from a bulb."

Don't spend your time correcting. Tune in and listen. Learn to enjoy the expressions of their wonder years.

Parent Preparation

At first, children will overgeneralize; they may see a cat, cow or collie and call each one a "doggy." Avoid the temptation to make too many corrections. They'll soon make their own modifications. Gradually your children will learn to play cooperatively and share with others. Noticing these achievements and sharing your feelings will assure their reassurance. ("I liked the way you played with Jenny and shared your toys with her.") Sharing and cooperation are important skills for the youngsters to repeat over and over during this period. And patience is a skill you'll need to repeat over and over. Relax with your children. Enjoy life; it's not time to rush and push.

As you do things together, talk out loud about your thoughts. "Let's see; I can tell it's cold outside by the frost on the window. So I'll want to put on my coat to stay warm when I go outside." These words help your child to learn how to think through situations.

Crayons or felt-tip markers will eventually draw masterpieces on your walls, furniture and/or clothes. Many children will use these colors to mark their area.

If asked, "Why did you do that?" they will invariably respond, "I don't know."

Try to channel the coloring activity to a more acceptable surface. Firmly say, "Here, I know you like your pretty colors. From now on only color in your coloring book or on plain paper. If you color on the wall or something other than your paper, you'll have to go to time-out."

When your child brings you his artwork, avoid saying, "What is this?" Instead say, "There are lots of pretty colors here. Tell me about your drawing," or "Thanks for taking the time to draw me a picture. I appreciate your thinking of me," or "This looks great—tell me about it." During the child's early years it's important for parents to spend time with their child. Do things with the child—have fun. These hours of time will be an investment in the future. Try doing the following activities with your child on a regular basis:

going for a walk
reading a story
wrestling on the floor
being silly
working a puzzle
taking pictures
going for a ride
singing songs
looking at the family album
praying together

Regardless of how you decide to spend the time, try to invest a minimum of forty-five to ninety minutes a day with each child. Sound reasonable? Time yourself for one week! Keep a daily record. You may be surprised.

Remain Flexible

Roger remembers one morning when he was driving Lane to nursery school. Just as Lane was about to get out of the car, Roger realized Lane had forgotten his lunchbox. Even mean old Dad wasn't yet ready to let a five year old miss lunch, especially since he had a very light breakfast.

"I'll go get your lunch box and bring it back. You go on in to school," Roger said.

95

"I want to ride home with you and then come back," Lane replied.

By this time his teacher was holding the car door open, and other parents were lined up in their cars, waiting to drop their children off.

"No, son, you go on in to school," Roger repeated, "and I'll bring your lunch to you."

"Please let me go with you, Dad," and he started to tear up.

By then Roger was getting upset because he thought Lane was stalling him.

"You can do it the easy way or the hard way, son, but either way you're going on in to school," Roger said, firmly.

With tears in his eyes and a dirty look on his face, he went inside. It was then that Roger had the "Aha!" esxperience.

As he drove back home to get the lunch box, Roger realized what the fuss was all about. Lane simply wanted to be with him; nursery school was not the issue. In Roger's rush to get things done "right," he lost sight of the fact that this was nursery school; they don't give you detentions or fail you for being late. The real issue was that Lane wanted to spend some more time with his father. What would have happened if he had stayed with Roger in the car while he returned for the lunch box? He would have missed about twenty minutes of nursery school, they would have avoided an unnecessary confrontation, and they could have spent more of that special time together.

Sometimes it's easy to get the cart before the horse in this parenting business. While trying to be straightforward and in charge, Roger became bound by his own system. As your child grows up, remember: "It's always important to be flexible." The world won't come to an end just because your routine needs to be modified.

Traveling with Small Children

A little planning can ease the tension of traveling with a

small child. Try:

1. Putting together a car activity bag with books, paper, stickers, card games, a cassette recorder and favorite tapes, and a special treat or a surprise toy.

2. Giving each child a small "Trip Treats" bag. Then each time the kids fight or argue, each of them is to give you one treat out of their bags. At the end of the trip, the remaining treats are theirs to keep.

3. Assembling a snack kit for the car. You should include a plastic cup, a small spoon, a bib, Wet-Ones, crackers, fruit, a dry washcloth and a few small trash bags.

4. Planning rest stops about every two hours.

5. Letting off energy and getting the circulation going by doing impromptu exercises at a roadside park.

6. Traveling fewer than eight hours in a day.

When Parents Are Gone for the Night

At times a parent will have to be gone overnight. Make preparations for the child before you leave by:

1. Recording at least one story for each night you'll be away. On a cassette tape read from one of your child's favorite books so he can follow along. Hearing an absent parent's voice is reassuring. At the end of the story say, "Good night, I'll see you again at home in [X] days."

2. If possible, have a relative or trusted sitter care for the child in your home to minimize a change in surroundings and routine. If the child is taken to a relative's home, write out a familiar routine and let your child bring one bag of toys.

3. Whatever the reason for leaving, tell your child, "A mom's supposed to come back for her child, and I'll come back to you too." After you return, remind your child, "Remember that I said I'd come back? Well, here I am." This kind of experience builds your child's confidence that absences aren't forever. Naturally the routine of bringing home a special gift

doesn't hurt, but you need to be cautious or else your child will come to expect the "gift" out of habit.

Tattling

When your child begins tattling try this, "There are two things that you should tattle about. Remember them:

"One, tell me anytime someone might get hurt doing what they are doing. It's OK to tell me, even if you get called names. And, two, tell me anytime someone might hurt you.

"You may be tempted to tell about other kinds of things, but just remember our two rules."

Are You Ready for Pets?

Here's how it went in one family. When Mindy was three years old, the subject of pets came up, and Mom mentioned that "one day" we'd get Mindy a kitten. Right away she started saying, "How soon?" So Mom picked a safe date out of the air, "Next year, when you're four years old." To a four-year-old little girl that sound like a long time, but was it long enough for her to forget the promise? Instead of forgetting, Mindy "memory keyed" *kitten* to "fourth birthday," and when the long-awaited birthday arrived, the "hounding" began, "Where's the kitten you promised?"

Fortunately, Mindy's birthday came in November, so Mom and Dad could say with some conscience, "We need to wait until spring when the weather is warmer." Mindy gave in, but soon it was spring.

One spring evening Dad brought home a cute little female kitten. Mindy named her "Socks." Both Mindy and Socks were excited at first, but soon Mindy was in tears. "Socks doesn't want to play with me. She won't let me hold her." Within three days Mindy had all but forgotten about Socks. The logical consequence was that Socks got less and less attention from everybody except Mom—Mom provided the Meow Mix.

Getting Socks was a mistake. Probably a stuffed kitten or a goldfish would have been better. Pets teach us a lot about life, but they teach only when our children are old enough to learn.

Managing Aggression

During the early childhood years, parents are often surprised with sudden bursts of aggression in the youngsters. We find ourselves wondering where such a sweet child gets this preoccupation with fighting and hitting. Around age three many children go through a bug-squashing phase in which any and all ants, worms and caterpillars they come across are subject to being flattened on sight. Sometimes a child will try to flatten another child. Usually, just feelings are hurt. Avoid making too big of a deal about it.

Biting

When biting gets out of hand, you might use negative practice by sending your child to a time-out corner and have him bite down on a washrag for three minutes until the timer goes off. Some people will tell you to encourage the injured child to bite back, but that only teaches that one bad turn deserves another instead of eliminating future biting. Punish the guilty party; don't teach the innocent how to be a biter.

Fussing and Fighting

Fussing and fighting are typical problems common to almost all small children. If they never fussed, we would wonder what was wrong with them. As long as the fussing and fighting are about the normal childhood things and at normal levels, we suggest letting kids solve their own problems without adults getting involved. Occasionally things will get out of hand, and you'll need to step in.

A low-intensity situation is demonstrated by arguing or verbal fighting. Whenever two children are fussing back and forth and the noise level gets out of hand or the threats become a little too vivid, simply say, "Look, I don't know what all the fussing and arguing is about, but I do know I don't like the noise. I'll tell you what—you have one minute to settle this yourselves quietly and work out your own solution. If you don't settle this in one minute, I'm going to come back in here and give you my solution. And I guarantee that my solution will work. Now you have one minute to settle this quietly." Walk out of the room.

Most children will quickly come up with some creative solutions if you just offer them the opportunity to do so and make it uncomfortable if they don't. It doesn't matter if one decides to yield to the other and "give in," because yielding is useful to learn early in life, especially before kids start riding their bikes in the street. Don't worry about yielding becoming lopsided. If it does and one child does all the yielding, pretty soon he'll get tired of it and will insist on reciprocity.

If your kids don't solve their problem after one minute and are still arguing, simply come in and give them your solution which might be, "Time-out for you in that corner, and time-out for you over there." If they continue to fuss or nag, say, "I'm adding one minute for each time you fuss." Then walk out after setting the timer.

Fistfights and Wrestling

A high-intensity situation is identified by physical fighting. It can be handled by making your child shadow box in a corner or hold weights or rocks for three minutes. (The arms will get tired real fast.) Most will be worn out before the time is up. If one of the two says, "It wasn't my fault," tell him, "You need to learn to avoid getting into fights. Just because someone dares you to fight is no reason to fight back. This way I make sure the responsible one is punished." If you are certain that one child deliberately goaded the other into a fight, you might give the guilty party a double portion of shadowboxing, while the other gets a regular portion for fighting back. One punch in self-defense is one thing, a prolonged fight is another.

Some parents think they should let the kids fight it out to the end. You use your judgment. You may find a tooth gone and a few bruises. Other parents believe if one child hits another the innocent should be able to hit the guilty one back twice. The problem with that is the same as with biting back. Besides, the innocent party will rarely hit the guilty one hard enough to do any good. Usually the innocent are too shy, intimidated or afraid to take the necessary action. The shadowbox routine is more useful.

Playing Sick

Children sometimes use illness and complaints of being sick to avoid doing something they don't want to do. It's a convenient excuse to keep from leaving a parent's side or going to Sunday school or nursery school. When you feel that your child is faking and his temperature and other signs look all right, respond to his complaints this way: "If you're really sick, I understand, and of course you don't have to go. If you are too sick to go to nursery school, then you'll need to stay in your pajamas all day so you can rest and get well and go back to school soon.

"The only exceptions to staying in bed will be to go to the bathroom and to come to the table to eat, if you feel like it. If you get to feeling better after school lets out, you'll still need to stay in bed and rest to avoid a 'relapse' just in case." If the child is faking, you will find him getting well—fast!

Relieving Fears

Technically speaking, many of the common childhood fears might be considered phobias. While they may be irrational or highly unlikely to come true ("There's a bear in my room"), to the child these are real events, and making light of such fears is counterproductive. Parents can help children overcome any fear by teaching them ways to solve their own problems.

If your child is afraid of outside noises, avoid saying, "They're only noises." Instead, explain what makes the noise: "When the wind blows the tree and the tree rubs against the house, it sounds like this," and show the child how such a noise is produced by rubbing two of his toys together. If possible, take your child outside: "Would you like to go see how the tree makes that noise?" If your child is too scared to do so, practice making the noise. Show him how he can make the noise by mimicking it. Once he can produce a similar sound, he'll have more control over it.

Since most children's fears are based on imaginary facts, an imaginary solution will often work. When your child is convinced that there is a bear in the closet, ask him if he would rather shoot it or hit it over the head and knock it out. Shooting seems to be the action of choice for boys.

Then get some imaginary guns. Have your child lead you to exactly where the bear is. Ask your child to get ready to shoot as you turn on the lights. Then turn on the lights and listen for your child to shoot. Then talk about how glad you are that that's over. Check the bear to see if it's dead and pretend to drag it out of the room.

What an adventure you have had. Now the bear is gone and your own child is the hero. Sweet dreams.

Nightmares

All children have bad dreams from time to time. Persistent bad dreams or nightmares may come from a friend who tells scary stories. It may have been some bad news on TV (and there's plenty of that). Or it may have been any number of circumstances. It's useless to tell a child, "It's all in your head." That's just the point—our dreams *are* in our head. The child knows it, and he becomes scared of going to sleep because he fears another nightmare. It's rather like an adult who is reluctant to take a boat ride because he gets seasick easily. There's some justification for the reluctance.

Your child may need you to wait in his room for several nights until he goes to sleep. I discourage rocking an older child, over two years of age, to sleep because it can become a habit, making rocking necessary for sleep. Lying on a pallet beside your child's bed until he goes to sleep can be helpful. Usually this takes no more than 15 minutes and it gives us a chance to relax, pray together, and talk quietly for a moment. It's a small thing to do that can comfort your child a lot.

If your child's nightmares haven't diminished after two weeks of using these suggestions, or if he frequently wakes up screaming, professional intervention is probably called for. Ask your child's pediatrician for advice about what to do next.

Serious Illness

Roger once worked with a child whose father had been hospitalized unexpectedly with severe health problems. Eight-year-old Joey was told nothing about the nature of his father's illness, only that Dad was taken by ambulance to the hospital for several weeks. During that time, the rest of the family walked on pins and needles lest they upset and scare Joey.

Unfortunately, their behavior did exactly that. It was obvious to Joey that something was going on, and for some reason his relatives weren't leveling with him. He decided something must have been very wrong with his father because no one bothered to tell him.

When a close relative is in the hospital or when someone

103

dies, it is imperative for parents to tell their children the truth in a manner appropriate to the child's age and understanding. A rule of thumb is this: If a child is old enough to formulate a question, then he's old enough to receive an appropriate answer. Gory details should be omitted, but a simple, straight-forward answer will work wonders for a child's peace of mind. Not knowing is almost always worse than knowing. If a child is patronized or ignored during a time of sickness or sorrow, he'll assume that he may be at fault or that things are worse. Then his fears will really skyrocket, like Joey's did. Even small children have a fairly high tolerance for bad news if it's presented to them fairly, accurately and without undue alarm.

Typically children in this predicament assume the worst possible outcome. Rarely do we see children who erroneously concluded the best possible outcome. Tell children the truth on a level they can understand. Avoid fancy terms and jargon. Just say, "He's real sick," instead of "He has spinal meningitis."

When Someone Dies

Children growing up today are more aware of the reality of death than you may realize, yet most parents shy away from discussing the end of life. Youngsters need simple and honest information about what has happened when someone dies. The facts will almost always be better than the fantasies dreamed up out of ignorance.

Making sure kids get good information reminds me of the story of Jimmy and his baby sister. Late one night Jimmy's little sister was rushed to the hospital in one of those cars with flashing red lights. Dad woke Jimmy up, and they followed the ambulance to the emergency room. There, after several tests, the doctor said that Jimmy's sister needed a blood transfusion. She had a very rare blood type, the same as Jimmy's. Dad bent down and asked if Jimmy would be willing to help his sister by giving her some of his blood. Jimmy looked stunned but eager, "Sure, Dad, I'll do it."

Dad returned to the doctor, and Jimmy turned to his mother and said, "Here, you keep my bear; I won't need it anymore. I'm going to give Sis my blood. I love you, Mommy." Jimmy thought giving blood meant he would have to die. He didn't have enough information, and what he had he didn't understand.

Preparing your child for a funeral or memorial service is extremely important even if the child does not attend. Explaining death and funerals and cemeteries to your child helps to dispel his fear and worry.

Don't tell your child that Granny died because God needed another angel. That sets your youngster up to be mad at God for taking his Granny. After all, God's got thousands of angels, and your child's only got one Granny.

Don't use words like "sleep" or "gone away" as an attempt to soften the harshness of death. These euphemisms will cause the child to fantasize about the loved one's return. When you are faced with the task of helping a three to five year old through the grief process, remember:

Shoot straight with the youngster. He will sense something wrong sooner than you think.

Tell the child as soon as it is appropriate; don't wait until the rest of the family has recovered. The child shouldn't have to grieve alone.

Talk about good memories of the deceased.

Hug your child lots.

Use simple but factual information in describing what happens or might happen at the funeral and cemetery.

Don't be afraid to cry. It's good to cry. Death is a sad time.

Security Blankets

Like Linus of Peanuts fame, many children get attached to a blanket, favorite stuffed toy or pillow, which they drag with them everywhere. These items become like a part of the child's body. Removing the blanket would be as painful as removing an arm; at least it seems that way.

This security blanket can become a major source of parental concern. "But what if she still wants it by the time she goes to school?" The point is, the blanket offers some degree of comfort and security or else it wouldn't be that important to the child to lug around everywhere. As long as it's offering that much comfort, I wouldn't try to get rid of it.

If you feel your child is about ready to give up the blanket but just doesn't know how to let go, make it easier for her. Suggest an alternate place to put the freshly laundered blanket, like in the linen closet. I know it's probably in shreds, but it is precious to your child and hard to let go of. Offer to clean it up, put it in a special plastic bag or box where she'll know it'll be safe from moths and where she can take it out or look at it anytime she might want to. Tell her it's starting to get worn and she might want to save it for her little girl or her little girl's dolls someday.

If that doesn't work, simply allow logical consequences to take place and let her take the blanket to kindergarten. Either a teacher will tell her it's against the rules and she'll probably comply, or the other kids will make enough fun of her for being a baby that she'll leave the blanket at home after a few days.

Thumb Sucking

Sucking thumbs seems to embarrass and irritate parents more than the sight of a security blanket. Like security blankets, it's usually a bigger problem for parents than for the child. If yours is still sucking his thumb and you think it's time for him to stop, you might ask if he's ready to stop now or if he wants to stop before school starts. If he's ready now, ask him if he wants you to remind him when he has his thumb in his mouth or would he rather receive stars on a chart for each time you see his mouth empty? If neither of these approaches works, I'd let logical consequences take their course.

Most thumb sucking is taken care of in the first three to four days of school by the other kids' taunts. If he's willing to with stand their ridicule, then the thumb must have precious security value for him, so I probably wouldn't try to take it away. Besides, there are lots of adults who suck on cigarettes; a thumb is much safer.

There are several chemicals and bandages available to apply to thumbs and fingers to deter sucking and nail biting. We have not found those to be effective long term, but they might be just the thing for the short term.

Bedtime Problems

Sooner or later all children will try to get in their parents' bed. Besides the security it offers, the parents' bed is usually warmer and has more room than the child's. Crawling in a parent's bed on Saturday mornings to snuggle is one thing, but it's not a good idea for children to sleep overnight in their parents' bed, even when one parent is gone. It's too easy for this to become a habit, and then the child will have trouble sleeping in his own bed. After a while, children who sleep in their parents' bed confuse their role in relation to their parents and may demand to remain in that bed, resenting the parent (usually Dad) who expects them to sleep in their own bed.

One way to encourage your child to sleep in his own bed is to offer him a star or check mark for each morning you wake up and find him in his own bed. It works even better if you let him make the marks. When he has earned five stars, let him select a special treat worth about one dollar. As he becomes more and more proficient at remaining in his own bed, increase the price for the treat from five to seven stars then to ten, etc.

Finally, phase the program out when the child has developed the habit of staying in his own bed. Of course, waking

107

up in his own bed means your child did not go into your room the night before and have to be brought back to bed by you. In such a case, he doesn't get a star the next morning. If he asks why not, explain why. This procedure has worked quite well for a number of parents.

Nightly Routines

It helps to have an established routine each night. One family used an old-fashioned, wind-up alarm clock, the kind with two bells on top. It was called Mr. Clock, and whenever bedtime drew near the parents called out, "It's time to wind up Mr. Clock." Their kids raced to be the first one to wind up Mr. Clock. Each got a turn winding the alarm key. Then their parents set the alarm to go off in about ten minutes. The children knew from experience they only had a brief amount of time to brush their teeth, get a last-minute book or toy, get a hug and kiss from Mom and Dad, and then off to bed.

When Mr. Clock's alarm went off, ready or not there was no further running around, but, "Off to bed you go." Mom and Dad came in with them to say prayers and tuck them in.

Routines and rituals are important for children. The more you establish a set time and routine for going to bed, the easier it will be for your children and you. At first it takes practice and patience to establish the routines, but they're well worth the effort.

The main thing about bedtime and nap time for preschool children is that your child stays in bed quietly without disturbing the rest of the family. If you allow her the freedom to read or talk quietly to her sister or stuffed animals, most will soon relax and fall asleep in about fifteen minutes.

Distractions at Bedtime

Occasionally a child will have such a large collection of stuffed animals on the bed that sleeping seems impossible.

Before you intervene and remove the animals, ask yourself, "Does she seem to sleep in a restful manner, and does she seem rested when she wakes up?" If so, there's probably no problem. Some of us can't imagine how others can sleep on a waterbed or an extra-firm bed, but many do. On the other hand, if your child is obviously not rested when she wakes up, start reducing the number of animals she's allowed in bed by one each night until she wakes up rested.

Tell her, "Tonight you can have eleven animals" (or whatever number you want to start with) "in bed with you." First, remove the three-feet-tall gorilla or any others that are huge. If she doesn't wake up rested the next morning, keep reducing the number by one each night until she does. In less than a week you'll probably have the number down pat. If she refuses to select which animals she wants to start with, tell her, "All right, since you seem to have trouble choosing, I'll make the selection for you." Be sure to leave her favorites with her. Don't allow any trades to be made, or she'll just delay you in a trade-off game to prolong going to bed.

Avoid any activity near bedtime that gets a child wound up, like wrestling, tickling or playing chase. Choose slow-down activities instead, like reading bedtime books, softly singing gentle songs and saying prayers together. Make sure the TV is off and the lights are turned down. Leave the nightlight on and have the bed ready for your child. If you choose to read books, decide how many to let your child select, and then it's time for bed.

When Parents Disagree

Parents often ask us about being consistent with children. How important is consistency? It would be nice if parents always agreed on everything, but that just doesn't happen. It makes more sense for each parent to be as consistent as possible in his/her own form of discipline so kids will learn predictability.

109

It can be very helpful to work through a disagreement in front of your children and let them see a solution process, unless the problem is about your personal life or something that's clearly not the children's business. When the problem at hand has to do with them, they can watch and even be included in the discussion if it's appropriate.

What can you do if a child hears you arguing and asks you to stop?

Kneel down beside him and say, "Son, Mom and Dad have a problem right now that we need to work out. We're going to talk about it until we get a good solution. You can stay here and listen, but not interrupt us, or you can play in your room or in the backyard. Either way, we'll keep working on this problem until we have a happy solution."

When children hear parents disagree behind closed doors and then later come out with a "solution," all they may learn is that parents are supposed to "hide" when they have problems. You can't hide your feelings. All children are perceptive and somewhat intuitive. They sense the disturbance in your heart, and they will always imagine the worst. It's best to let them observe two mature adults creating a solution.

A Typical Day with Common Sense Discipline

Here are some typical situations where common sense discipline can be applied:

Getting Up: "If you get up, get dressed and eat breakfast in a good mood, you'll get one star on your chart. When you have five stars you can have a dollar or pick a toy that costs that much."

After Breakfast: "I enjoyed breakfast with you. It was fun talking about our plans for the day. Now please go wash your hands and face, and then we will play one game together."

"I want to play now, Mommy."

"No, you know your routine. After you eat, you wash your

hands and face; then we play. Now hop to it!"

When it comes time to stop playing a game, children often have a hard time quitting abruptly, so give notice like: "I can take three more turns, and then I'll need to go back to my work. You can keep playing here, or you can join me in the kitchen." Count the remaining turns out loud, "That's one. . .that's two. . ." and then return to your work.

Later That Morning: "I'm ready for a little break. I sure appreciate the way you've been playing quietly and letting me do my work. That sure does help me. How about we play one of your games for a few minutes now?"

Lunch Time: "When you finish your lunch you can have dessert." Note: This doesn't mean lick the plate clean, just a normal portion of food.

"But I don't want to eat this food."

"That's fine. Only eat it if you want dessert."

"But I want my dessert now."

"No, and if you nag me again you'll have to go stand in the time-out corner for three minutes."

Nap Time: "We have time for one story or one quiet game before nap time. You can pick. When we're finished it will be time to take a nap."

After Nap Time: "You took a good nap. I bet you feel rested." If you've been doing your work and your child wants to play, you might say, "I need to finish what I'm doing first. I'll set the timer to remind me to stop in fifteen minutes. Then you and I can play a game you pick for fifteen minutes so you'll get a turn to play. When the timer goes off, I'll have to go back to my work. You can keep playing, or you can watch one TV show we agree on."

After Dinner: "Tonight you need to take a bath. After you're all dried off and have your pajamas on, we'll straighten up the bathroom together. Then after you brush your teeth, I'll read a story, and then it will be bedtime."

Avoid getting trapped by all of the usual arguments.
"But I don't want to."
"You don't have to want to. You just have to."
Then start filling the bathtub.

CHAPTER 7
Helping Kids Learn Self-Control

6-11 Years

BY THE TIME YOUR CHILDREN REACH school age, most of us have long since given up the hope of raising perfect children. In fact, most of us have done or said a few of those things that we vowed we would never do or say. Kids have a way of testing us and humbling us. This testing and humbling can become a game, a competition of wills. One of the results of playing this game and losing is "The G.A.S. Trap." Without knowing why or how they're doing it, some kids learn to use Guilt, Anger, and Silence to get their way.

The GAS Trap

Guilt   (Stage 1)
Anger   (Stage 2)
Silence   (Stage 3)

The GAS trap usually moves in sequence from Stage 1 to Stage 3, and it's been my experience that the trap gets tighter as you move from stage to stage. On occasion a kid will skip guilt and start with anger or silence, but you still feel guilty. The goal in any case is to win!

The Guilt Trip

Children are great organizers of guilt trips, so Stage 1 often begins like this: "Mom/Dad, if you won't let me do such-and-such activity or buy me this or that, all of the other kids will make fun of me, and I'll be the only one left out. So please, p-l-e-a-s-e!?" As soon as you start feeling just the least bit guilty and thinking that maybe you aren't such a good parent after all, you have begun the guilt trip.

Many of us have been conditioned to try to give our kids whatever they ask for. Parents who are conditioned like this have difficulty seeing the difference between wants and needs. I heard one man quote Matthew 7:9-11 as his reason for trying to fulfill all requests: "Which of you, if his son asks for bread, will give him a stone? Or if he asks for a fish, will give him a snake? If you, then, though you are evil, know how to give good gifts to your children, how much more will your Father in heaven give good gifts to those who ask him!"

Stop and think for a moment—has God given you everything you've asked for? Has he asked you to wait for some things? Has He said no to others? Isn't it all right then to say no to your kids and not feel guilty about it? Say something like, "Well, I know it's no fun to be left out, but I just don't think what you're asking for is a good idea, so I'm going to say no."

Fits of Anger

After a few more attempts to get you to bite down on the guilt bait, they'll proceed to Stage 2, Anger. "I can't stand you! All the other kids say I have the meanest parents, and I tried to stand up for you, but now I know they're right. I hate you!"

Anger is a very natural emotion. When it is used to express

the feelings of the moment, then it's a legitimate way to share our hurt and frustration. Anger is like a smoke detector that warns us we have a problem. The anger says loud and clear that something has caused hurt or frustration. When anger is used to attack, however, it becomes a weapon, and its design is to get someone to change his mind.

When your child uses an anger attack, say something like, "Sorry you feel that way, but if you change your mind, please let me know." About this time he'll storm off down the hall, loudly slamming the door to his room for emphasis, just in case you didn't get the message that he's mad. He wants to win!

The Silent Treatment

Stage 3, Silence, starts as the parent goes down the hall after their kid, quietly knocking on the door lest he upset this frail bundle of nerves any further, and says, "Hon, can we talk? Hon, are you in there? Now, don't be mad." (That was his intent, remember?) "Can we talk?" (Don't hold your breath.) Then the parent opens the door a crack and peers timidly in. The youngster is on the bed, music blasting, eyes teared, mouth closed and, whether the parent knows it or not, ears tuned into another world. Remember, the kid is getting ready to win, so he is listening for the thrill of victory. Listen, you'll build igloos in Miami before that iceberg melts, so leave it alone for a while. Time and warmth always melt ice.

Next time your kid storms off down the hall, consider it a good omen because then you'll have about two hours to read a book, watch what you want on TV, take a hot bath, or even take a nap. So enjoy your time. Besides, no fish ever got caught but what bit the bait. Recognize GAS traps for what they are, guilt-loaded tricks that all kids learn to use while still quite young. If they didn't use GAS from time to time, then folks like us would probably wonder what was wrong. So cancel the guilt trip. Your child may offer you the tickets, but you don't have to go along for the ride.

When a child says, "I hate you," avoid the temptation to say, "Oh, no, you don't!" All people, even grade school children, have intense emotional experiences at times. To tell a child, "You don't feel that way" either denies the child's experience or says you can't handle a tense situation, neither of which you want to convey. It's one thing to joke when a kid's giving you GAS, but when the emotion is real, then sit down and talk about, "What is it about me that you hate?" If you're willing to keep the conversation going without getting defensive, you'll probably have a very productive talk.

If your child gets angry and says, "You're the meanest mom in the world!" shrug your shoulders and say, "Thanks, I've always wanted to be famous for something. I guess that makes you famous, too! Now, what's the real problem?"

GAS and the Stepparent

Stepchildren may be more adept at pumping GAS than most. On weekend visits stepparents are hit with statements like, "You're not my real mother. I don't have to do that when I'm at my real home." The best response for this is something like, "You're ever so right. I know I'm not your *real* mother, but I am your *real* father's *real* wife, and that makes me part of this family, so get with the program." If both natural parents are around, children have to learn to live in two different homes. Sometimes parents will use the kids as weapons to get back at their ex. Stepchildren will take advantage of this situation by using the casketlike GAS trap. It'll seem like there's no way out alive.

Stepchildren are quick to point out the variation in rules between their two households, "But that's not the rule at my real mother's house."

"That's fine, George. When you're at your real mother's house, we expect you to go by her rules, and when you're at our house, we expect you to go by our rules. I know that's tough, but I know you can handle it without any problem."

Stepparents play a special role in a child's life, yet there is no possible way they can ever be fully prepared for the stepparenting experience. Your spouse's children from a previous marriage will always be a part of your present marriage in some fashion. The sooner you accept that fact the better for all concerned.

Common Sense Discipline Chart 4

Chart 4 suggests that during the grade school years children are capable of more and more personal decisions. The experiences of these years provide children the opportunity to be responsible for their schedules, their homework, their rooms, and their friends. These responsibilities involve major decisions, and that's the way it should be.

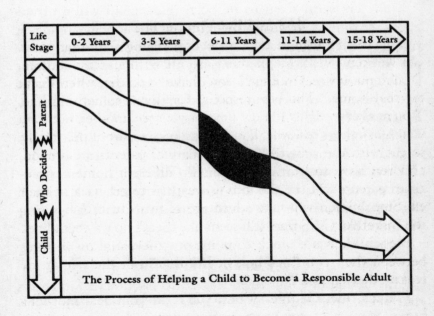

117

Three Critical Lessons

During your child's first three school years, each day is a new experiment in the laboratory of life. At school the kids learn basics like read'n, 'rit'n and 'rithmetic—the three Rs of education. At home the curriculum is more practical. Parents are the teachers of how to grow up—the three Rs of life: reliability, resourcefulness and responsibility. These "grown-up" qualities take years to develop, but they must take root during the grade school years.

Reliability

A reliable child will learn to complete chores and follow instructions on his own. Rules and limits help him to know what to do and when to do it. Schedules and daily routines help him organize activities so he remembers and completes them on his own.

Resourcefulness

Some children seem to be born resourceful while others appear at times to have all the lights on, but nobody's home. A resourceful child will take charge of his own life and solve problems as they arise. No longer is there a need for constant adult supervision. In fact, a resourceful youngster likes to be free to develop his own interests and work on them on his own.

Responsiblity

Children are genetically programmed to be responsible— someday! A responsible child takes care of his room, his clothes, his possessions, and himself (although not necessarily in that order). He begins to enjoy caring for others, too. Each day he seems to be more and more aware that he is programmed for independence.

Suzy and the Three Rs

The mother of a fourth grader was deeply troubled. It seems that sweet little Suzy refused to take a bath unless Mom ran the tub for her. Then Suzy would complain until Mom

118

scrubbed her back. Suzy wouldn't get dressed unless Mom laid out her clothes. Of course, Mom's selections were never the right ones. Suzy's responsibility program seemed to be on hold, resourcefulness was questionable, and reliability was out to lunch. Mom was at the end of her frazzled rope. She asked:

"What can I do? She refuses to take a bath unless I scrub her back, and then she won't go to school unless I take her in the car."

"How far is it to the school?" the counselor asked.

"Four blocks."

"How do the other kids in your neighborhood get to school?"

"They walk or ride their bikes."

"What would happen if you let Suzy get to school on her own?"

"She'd probably be late, because she waits until the very last minute because she knows I'll have to take her."

"Have to take her?" I said incredulously.

"Well, if I didn't, she'd be tardy because she waits so long."

"Uh huh. And then what would happen if she came to school tardy?"

"Well, I guess she'd get a detention and have to stay after school."

"Uh huh, and how long do you think Suzy would allow that to happen before she decided to get going on time to avoid being tardy again?"

"OK, I think I see what you mean. Well, I could let her be tardy, but still she'd wear the most outlandish clothes if I didn't select some for her."

"I know that's embarrassing, but if the clothes were really inappropriate, what would her teachers do?"

"They'd probably send her home and make her serve a detention for the classes she missed."

"OK, what do you think would happen if you quit cooperating with her stalling routine and stopped drawing her bath and scrubbing her back? They don't even give that kind of service in expensive hotels, so why do you do it at home?"

"Well, if I didn't make her take a bath, she'd probably go to school smelling bad."

"Uh huh, and how long do you think it would be before the other kids or teachers said something to her about it?"

"Oh, OK. In other words, you think she's old enough to learn to take care of this by herself, or suffer the consequences?"

"Bingo. If she's smart enough to figure out how to manipulate you, the adult who's supposed to be in charge here, then she's certainly smart enough to figure out how to be responsible, resourceful, and self-reliant."

Your Plan for Children with Self-Discipline

Don't let a few disappointments destroy your confidence as a parent. Your child didn't learn to walk without falling down, and he won't grow up without messing up. Hebrews 10:32-36 sounds like it was written just to help parents hold on to their confidence.

> Remember those earlier days after you had received the light, when you stood your ground in a great contest in the face of suffering. Sometimes you were publicly exposed to insult and persecution; at other times you stood side by side with those who were so treated. You sympathized with those in prison and joyfully accepted the confiscation of your property, because you knew that you yourselves had better and lasting possessions. So do not throw away your confidence; it will be richly rewarded. You need to persevere so that when you have done the will of God, you will receive what he has promised.

Learning to be reliable, resourceful and responsible takes years of living. Don't expect these lessons to be learned without your share of difficult times. Although there are no magic potions that will guarantee success, you will discover a deep reservoir of self-confidence if you have a plan. Turning your home into a laboratory of life demands some kind of lesson plan. It is God's will that you "train a child in the way he should go" (Proverbs 22:6), and all training requires a plan of action.

A successful plan of action will help your child develop reliability, resourcefulness, and responsibility while you are becoming more self-confident. As a bare minimum, your plan must have these seven steps:

1. Talk It Out
2. Get Inside Their Heads
3. Make the Rules
4. Break It Down
5. Show Them How
6. What Will Happen
7. Did It Work?

Developing your plan will also rescue you from the GAS trap!

1. Talk It Out

The first step in helping your child to develop the reliability, resourcefulness, and responsibility that Suzy didn't have is spending time talking with child. Talking gives you the opportunity to (1) get to know what he is thinking and feeling, (2) set and discuss appropriate rules of behavior, and (3) share your expectations.

2. Get Inside Their Heads

At times asking questions is the only way to get information. Some kids will never voluntarily tell you anything about what's going on inside their heads. Try a family interview night. It can be fun, interesting and very informative. Use questions like:

Who is your favorite teacher?

If you could have any wish granted, what would it be?

What sport do you enjoy the most?

Who is your greatest hero?

How do you know God is listening to your prayers?

What embarrasses you the most?

Who is your best friend?

What really makes you angry?

What is the best gift you have ever received?

What do you think God does all day?

What is your favorite song?

How do you act when you are really angry?

Where would you like to go for vacation?

What is your biggest fear?

What is something you are good at?

What kind of job do you want to have when you grow up?

What do you think heaven will be like?

How do you like doing these interviews?

Make a family video; these responses may change from year to year and a video will give you a great record of your child's growth. It can be lots of fun too.

3. Make the Rules

Every family has rules. Every family needs rules. Tell the following story, and ask your child to make up his own ending.

Once there was a king in a small country who was very unhappy. He had to listen to all the cases where the people broke the law. This kept him very busy all day long, so he got very tired of all the people breaking the law. One day he thought, "I wonder what it would be like if there were no laws? If there are no laws then there would be no lawbreakers, and I would have no cases to listen to all day." So he decreed that beginning tomorrow people could do anything they

wanted to. There would be no more law. The next
day. . .

This story will help you discuss the need for rules. The bottom line is that rules work only if the children know what the
rules are. Get the kids together and make a list of the rules in
your family. You will find that you probably have rules on the
following subjects:
bedtime
homework
toys
television
food
play
clothes
work
speech
friends

Rules should be simple and positive. They are meant to
help people, not hurt people. After you have brainstormed
your list of rules, vote on the ten most important ones.

Discussions like this help your children to see the need for
the rules your family has adopted. Then as you make more rules
about behavior, the kids will have an easier time accepting the
rules without getting exasperated. When rules are discussed
they tend to be remembered, and you may even hear your kids
say, "That's the way we do it at our house!" instead of "That's
the dumb rule my parents made up!"

4. Break It Down

Learning to be responsible does not happen in one "super
lesson." Responsibility is developed bit by bit. Don't expect a
clean room all at once. A job that big must be learned a little
at a time. If you want your child to keep his room neat, first let
him have responsibility for taking his dirty clothes to the laun-

dry room. Then later he can work on vacuuming, dusting, and washing woodwork.

Charts help children develop reliability, resourcefulness and responsibility in an organized way. There are three basic types of charts that can be used:

Assignment Chart

This chart names household tasks and helps children remember who does each job.

	MORNING	EVENING
SUSAN	GAMEROOM	ASSISTANT COOK
ERIC	FAMILY ROOM	SET TABLE
TIM	BATHROOM	EMPTY DISHWASHER
JULIE	FRONT ROOM	TRASH

Fun Charts

You can use these charts creatively to help the child discover the enjoyment and satisfaction of work.

DECORATE THE TREE

AN APPLE FOR EACH BOOK.

PICK A JOB

Incentive Charts

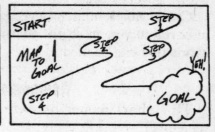

NAMES	DATE	DATE	DATE	DATE	DATE	DATE
SUSAN	★					
ERIC			★		★	
TIM				★		
JULIE		★				★

These charts use checks, stars, or stickers to show the child's accomplishment and progress. Using charts positively can help your child to grow up. Charts work for these five reasons:

Charts help us learn a task a step at a time.

Charts put some excitement in the routine.

They foster a sense of fairness—the child knows exactly what is expected; there are no surprises.

Charts help children to think in an orderly fashion.

Charts can become a source of incentive to complete the task at hand.

5. Show Them How

Teaching your youngster how to do something new is one of the most meaningful things a parent can do, and it is a powerful way to build your child's self-esteem. You are the most significant teacher your children will ever have. Think of all the things your youngster has learned from you: talking, walking, eating, dressing, throwing, hugging, building, cooking, trusting, and fishing, just to name a few. Let me tell you about fishing.

It was six o'clock Saturday morning when Ryan was awakened by Dad's familiar voice, "Ryan, it's time to get ready!" Ryan jumped to his feet, ran to the bathroom, put on his clothes and scurried into the kitchen holding his Nikes.

Dad looked at his watch, "Two minutes, that's a record! Are

125

you ready to catch a record trout?"

"You bet I am. Where's my pole?" Ryan said after tying his last shoelace.

"I put everything in the trunk," Dad said. "Let's go! First stop, McDonald's."

After a quick breakfast, the two adventurers drove to the river, parked the car and began getting ready for the hike down to the river.

"Remember," Dad said, "you need to stay close by me while we're at the river. Here's your pole, and here's mine. Do you still know how to use the reel?"

"Uh huh, but show me again."

Dad stood behind Ryan putting his hand on his son's seven-year-old inexperienced hand and demonstrated the casting and the reeling.

"I think you're ready. Show me you can do it by yourself."

Dad knew he could, and Ryan did. After reeling in the line, they headed down the mountain to the river. It was going to be the best day ever.

They fished for three hours and didn't catch a fish. Ryan followed Dad everywhere. He tangled his line only twelve times, he fell in the water twice, he lost his cap and cut his knee—but he had learned to cast! A slightly disappointed and tired boy followed his dad up the trail to the car. He put his pole in the trunk without a word and climbed into the front seat.

As they drove off, Dad said, "I hope you're not too disappointed that we didn't catch any trout."

Ryan reached over, hugged Dad's leg and said, "It's OK, Dad. We'll get the trout next time."

Before Ryan drifted off to sleep, Dad asked, "What was the best part of the trip?"

Ryan barely managed to open his eyes, but without hesitation he replied, "The best part was doing what you did, except when I fell in. It was the best day ever."

Dad grinned and locked those words away forever.

Make sure you take the time to show your child how to do a task before you discipline the child for not doing it. Sometimes we forget.

6. What Will Happen

Just as it's important for our children to be shown how to do a required task, it is also important that they know exactly what will happen if they don't do it. We have already dealt with the basics of establishing consequences for misbehavior; now let's fine-tune a bit.

Imagine two sisters washing the dishes after dinner. This particular evening they are arguing between themselves concerning who is supposed to load the dishwasher and who is supposed to clean up the kitchen.

As the girls get louder and louder, Mom finally is fed up. "Since you girls are having so much trouble with this task, you can spend the evening washing every dish in the cabinet. Start now!"

Wow, how about overkill! This kind of consequence will breed resentment and bitterness. Let's try it again. . . As the girls get louder and louder, Mom finally is fed up. "Since you girls are having trouble with this task, you can take turns doing it alone. Tonight will be Julie's turn. Start now!"

By the way, if you make an overkill consequence in anger or out of a misunderstanding, correct it right then. Tell the child how you feel, and adjust the consequence as you see fit. You may be able to save yourself from a load of guilt. Good consequences build acceptance, while bad consequences build resentment and rejection. Living with the results of our actions is part of growing up. These consequences keep the outside in line while our child is developing reliability, resourcefulness and responsibility on the inside.

All kinds of incentives can encourage grown-up behavior.

Parents could use any or all of the following as incentives or rewards:

verbal strokes

personal notes

special certificates

privileges

favorite foods

challenges or bets

money

Even an unexpected reaction, like laughing or joking, can be an incentive.

7. Did It Work?

Every plan needs constant evaluation. One early morning conversation may lead you to a deeper level of confidence in your child's reliability, or watching your youngster play with a friend may show you a resourcefulness you have never seen before. Noticing your child outgrowing the charts may help you sense the new level of responsibility now present in him. This new information will require you to modify your plan of action, and that's good.

Sometimes evaluation results in recognizing that it's not working. This requires a different kind of change. For example, it is rather normal to find a little procrastination in all of our children. Some, however, have developed the habit of procrastinating. To deal effectively with this problem, you should ask three questions:

1. How can you tell if your child is a procrastinator? Look for:

Delays in starting tasks

Slowness in finishing tasks

Excuse making

Consistently messy work

Continual waiting for help

Expressions of boredom
Staying away when there's work to do
2. What could be the reason? Consider:
Fear of failure
Expectation of perfection
Overwhelming task
Nonchallenging task
Addiction to TV
Ignorance about the task
A pattern of uncompleted tasks
3. What are my options? Try:
Praising positive efforts however small they may be
Offering something new in the process
Adjusting the task to fit the child
Insisting on keeping at it until finished
Using charts to help build a pattern of success
Appealing to a sense of competition
Helping them to develop necessary skills

Are Your Expectations Realistic?

Although it seems complicated, helping kids learn to be reliable, resourceful, and responsible comes naturally—if we'll let it. Letting our children experience the consequences of their behavior will teach lessons that lectures will never touch.

Don't expect to develop a plan that works great the first time. Plans are good only if they are realistic, and sometimes it takes a little experience to get realistic. You should know your child better than anyone else, so trust your instincts and lean on the Lord.

Remember, the goal is to raise children who learn how to be responsible adults—they aren't adults yet!

CHAPTER 8
Solutions That Make Sense

6-11 Years

EVEN WITH THE BEST OF INTENTIONS and the best plan of action, problems still poke holes in our confidence. We desperately want to do right, but as Lewis Carroll suggests, we have to have a problem (do something wrong) before we can learn the solution (do what is right).

Alice: Where I come from, people study what they are NOT good at in order to be able to do what they ARE good at. Grown-ups tell us to find out what we did wrong and never do it again.

Mad Hatter: That's odd! It seems to me that in order to find out about something, you have to study it. And when you study it, you should become better at it. Why would you want to become better at something and then never do it again?

Alice: Nobody ever tells us to study the right things we do. We're only supposed to learn from the wrong things. But, we are permitted to study the right things other people do. And sometimes we're even told to copy them.

Mad Hatter: That's cheating!

Alice: You're quite right, Mr. Hatter. I do live in a topsy-turvy world. It seems like I have to do something wrong first in order to learn from that what not to do. And then, by not doing what I'm not supposed to do, perhaps I'll be right. But I'd rather be right the first time, wouldn't you?

Lewis Carroll, *Through the Looking Glass*

Although Alice would like to do things right the first time, she really does learn more by what she does wrong. When we face problems in our family, it's usually because someone has done something wrong. Pointing out what's wrong, however, will not solve the problem. To solve our problems we must make sure we know exactly what went wrong. We must learn from our mistakes what not to do. Then we must concentrate on the right things we do to solve the problem.

In other words, we can spend our time worrying about what went wrong, or we can knuckle down and figure out what right things we can do to fix it.

This chapter is filled with typical childhood problems that need no-nonsense solutions. Look for the solutions that are right for you.

Early Morning Tensions

The five minutes just before leaving for school has traditionally become the loudest five minutes in America. For decades, mothers from coast to coast have been recorded yelling these things:

"Hurry up! You're going to be late!"

"Did you brush your teeth?"

"Can't you leave each other alone?"
"You'd forget your head if it wasn't attached!"
"Eat your lunch today. Don't trade it away!"
"Come straight home—no goofing off!"

To solve the early morning tension time, divide the morning routine into specific tasks and help your youngster become responsible for each task one at a time. At the right time you might find it helpful to tell your child: "When the car-pool comes, I expect you to be ready. If you aren't, then I'll put the rest of your clothes in a paper bag and toss them in the back seat. You will have to finish dressing on the way to school. It's your choice."

You may have to toss the bag in the car once, but you'll never have to do it twice. If you have doubts about your child's readiness for this action, think about how old he was when he could remember the days, times, and channels of his favorite TV shows.

Should the problem continue, try this: "If you are late and miss your ride and I have to take you, it will cost you. For every minute you rob from me, it will cost you five minutes of playtime/TV time, starting this afternoon. So if you inconvenience me fifteen minutes, it's going to cost you 5 x 15—or seventy-five minutes. You decide if you want to be ready or not."

Haggling with Homework

Some parents gripe and nag at their kids, and the homework still doesn't get done. Others end up doing the homework for the child. Either way, the child does not learn to be responsible for his own assignments. Even though the child has his own desk, his own computer and his own encyclopedia, he may not have his own self-discipline. He may be just plain lazy.

Some children need additional incentives to encourage them to study harder and make good grades. If your child is doing poorly in school mainly because of laziness, try this:

1. Stop all nagging about study. Prepare yourself and your child for a change. This will put his grades squarely on his own back.

2. Provide some special incentives to make study worthwhile. You might say, "Look, it's important to me that you make better grades. I know it may be hard to do that, but I'm willing to make it worth your while. For each passing grade you bring home from now on, here's what you will get: In addition to the points you receive for grades, I'll give you five

	GOOD GRADE CHART		
GRADE	DAILY ASSIGNMENTS	WEEKLY TESTS	COURSE GRADES
A	3 points	9 points	$3
B	2 points	6 points	$2
C	1 point	3 points	$1

points for each half hour you study at home."

3. Before TV can be watched after school, the youngster must study thirty to ninety minutes each might (parent's choice, depending on each child's situation and needs).

4. Decide on a set time and place for study each day. Let your child pick the best time and place for him. Remember, no TV until the study time is up. To earn the points, the parent must see the child studying or see the results of his work.

5. The points earned in this incentive program can be saved and traded for special activities like trips, events or appropriate surprises. What would your child pick?

Resistance to Reading

Each of the ideas suggested below can kindle or rekindle

your child's interest in reading.

Collect brochures and booklets about your town. Suggest your child read the collection and make a list of the most interesting things in your city.

Watch the TV news and discuss the people and events that made news that day. Encourage your child to read a newspaper and/or magazine article about people or events in the news.

Ask your child to read *TV Guide* and look up the unfamiliar words.

Ask your child to select a magazine or newspaper story. Now comes the fun. Have your child search for the longest word in the story, the "grossest" word and the most exciting word.

When picking a library book, ask your child to read one page aloud and hold up one finger for every word he can't pronounce. After reading the page aloud, if five fingers are held up, the book is probably too hard—it will frustrate the child.

Take books on vacations. Books help fill free time in cars, at campsites, and in motel rooms.

Read aloud to your kids even though they can read for themselves. The kids will enjoy the closeness and security of your voice.

Remember, the most effective way to encourage your child to read is to read yourself. Avid readers tend to raise children who become avid readers.

Fears and Failures

Children, because of their limited knowledge of the world around them, have many kinds of fears. Some have one or two, and some collect dozens of them.

Ron remembers when he had a secret fear. He was eight years old. Each night at bedtime he would reluctantly crawl into bed praying that God would help him sleep through the night. He was comforted by having his four-year-old brother in the bed with him. Of course, the bedroom door was left wide open, and the bathroom light was always left on.

One night during a storm, his home suffered a temporary power failure. All the lights went out, including that precious bathroom light. It was as if he was awakened by the darkness. He stared intently into the lightless hallway. Strange noises and unfamiliar shadows put his imagination on edge.

Suddenly a seven-foot-tall cowboy appeared. He began slowly walking toward the youngster's bed. The boy was frozen with fear. This cowboy was dressed in full cowboy-type garb: ten-gallon hat, chaps, boots, and twin six-guns. The eight year old could see all these details in a pitch-dark room. By the time the cowboy reached the bedside, the boy was sweating fear. He could see the zombielike eyes of the intruder.

Finally Ron got the courage to yell as loud as he could. "Don't kill me! No!" The cowboy continued to stare at the boy until Mom entered the room, and—poof!—he was gone.

Ron's active imagination painted the details of shadows and produced a vivid experience that initiated a fear, not of cowboys, but a fear of waking up in the middle of the night.

We have talked to grade school children who are afraid of spiders, dogs, snakes, bees, and sharks. One boy is afraid to swim where fish are—they might bite him. Nine year olds have told of their fear of their daddy and mommy losing their jobs. Many children are scared to death that their parents might get a divorce and some, even at an early age, have developed a fear of failing.

The Fear of Trying

The fear that saddens us most is the fear of trying. Some children today are so terrified by failure that they do everything within their power not to try new things. Children with this problem find it difficult to believe in themselves. They become increasingly more dependent upon parents and other adults.

A child will be eager to try new things only as long as his feet are firmly set on the trusted threshold of his own home. The self-confidence needed to try new things is produced at home. There are four distinct ways to encourage this self-confidence.

1. Acceptance of Failure—"I want you to know that you can never mess up bad enough for me to stop loving you. Whether you become a president or a prisoner, I will always love you!"

2. Social Security—"You are a special part of this family; you belong here. Everybody has to belong somewhere, and you belong here!"

3. Repeat Successes—"I believe you are best at —————. I like to watch people do their best, so would you do it for me? Thank you, I love it!"

4. Assign Responsibility—"This is your task. Here is how you do it. Practice it. Once you can do it by yourself, it will be your responsibility in this family. If you don't do it, it won't get done!"

Failing in School

About a month before school let out for the summer a mother brought her fifth-grade son to Roger's office. She was distraught because it appeared he might fail. He wasn't doing his homework at all.

"What's wrong with allowing him to fail? Sounds like he wants to fail. Can't he make it up in summer school?"

"Yes, but we've planned a special trip to Mexico this summer, and the tickets have already been purchased. If we cancel our reservations now there will be a sizable penalty. It's our first vacation in years. I thought we were all looking forward to the trip."

Roger helped develop a plan of action. He told her son: "Billy, I understand you may fail the fifth grade. If you do, you'll need to repeat the grade in summer school. As you know, your folks have been worried sick [loaded with guilt] because they feel they'll have to cancel their vacation plans because of your summer school. We've worked out a way for your parents and sister to still get to go on their trip, though you may miss out." Now they had his attention.

Roger continued, "Your mom and I discussed making arrangements with Mrs. Jones who lives down the street from you. You'll stay at her house while your folks are gone, and Mrs. Jones will take you to summer school. Mom and Dad will pay her room and board for your expenses in advance. Of course, due to the extra expense you'll have to do extra work at your house and Mrs. Jones's house during the summer. Of course, if your grades come up and you pass, then you can still go on vacation with your family."

One week later at her follow-up visit, the mother said, "I don't believe it. We saw you on Thursday, and by Monday morning he had completed three major projects that were overdue. I just don't believe it!"

"You mean he cheated?" Roger asked.

"No, the work was all in his writing. I just don't know how he did it. He must have stayed up all night Friday night. Then he studied all day Saturday and most of Sunday except for church time."

As it turned out, the boy passed, and the entire family enjoyed their vacation together.

Great things can happen when you let children become responsible for the consequences of their own behavior.

Clothes, Closets, and Cooperation

You may find your grade schooler going through several

changes of clothes in a day. If he puts his clothes in the proper places, it wouldn't be such a problem, but since the parent usually does the laundry, then we have a problem.

To encourage your child to put his clothes back in the closet or in the proper place, this rule may help: "Before you can watch TV or play during the evening, you must straighten up your room by putting away all clothes in their proper places."

Ideas for Clothes Care

Look at the closet from the child's eye level. Use bright padded hangers (kids like them). Install clothes hooks in the closet. Make sure the closet pole is hanging within easy reach of your child.

Have a dirty-clothes bag, basket or box in the child's room. Perhaps you might have two: one for light-colored clothes and the other for dark colors.

Use plastic stacking bins for clothes organizers.

Show your child how to use the washing machine.

Have your child use a nylon or mesh laundry bag for socks—just toss the whole bag in the washer and dryer. He will be able to sort them himself.

Before bedtime have your child lay out clothes for the next day, including shoes. (There is more time to find lost shoes at night than just before school.)

Scattered Clothes

If your children enter the house doing a "strip act," dropping a coat here, a soccer shirt there, and school books in the kitchen, then it's time for action. Say: "If I have to pick up these things of yours, it will cost you! The price is five minutes of playtime or TV time for each thing of yours. I want you to learn to remember."

TV: Adopted or Adapted

In the last few years videos opened up a more controlled and wholesome way to use the TV in the home.

Ron recommends the following family movie titles:

Field of Dreams
The NeverEnding Story
The Man from Snowy River
The Little Mermaid
The Parent Trap
Beauty and the Beast
The Wizard of Oz
The Sound of Music

Several children's video series are proving to be very popular:

Adventures in Odyssey
McGee and Me
Quigley's Village

Carefully select the network TV shows your family watches and insist that certain shows are off limits.

Set aside a time for family shows that you watch as a family. When parents and children express their views about a program, everyone gains insights about the program and each other.

Include the children in decisions about what you will watch during the week. Select a special time each week when the TV log will be reviewed and marked for the week.

Don't use the TV as a baby sitter. There is more problem with what TV keeps us from doing as a family than with what it does to a family.

Ask your child to think of another title for the program or series you are watching. Vote on the best suggestion.

Have your child write a description or review of the program after viewing it. Keep these reviews to use in selecting favorite TV shows of the year for your family.

During a commercial break ask: "What will happen next?"

Ask your child to time the commercials during a show and give you the total at the end of the show.

Have your child draw a picture describing his feelings about a show; then discuss the picture.

Turn off the volume but leave the picture on. Ask your children to make up some funny new dialogue for the action on the screen.

Without placing limits on the use of TV in your family, you may find yourself adopting TV as a member of your family. That would be tragic.

When Meanness Hurts

Children learn how powerful words are by what happens when they use them. If a word like *stupid* gets people's attention, then children will say "stupid" when they want attention. The tragedy is that while words like *stupid*, *dumb*, *butthead*, and *geek* get attention, they also can do great damage.

These simple little words used in the right setting can destroy even the healthiest self-esteem. It does little good to pretend we're immune to the pain. No one likes being put down by others. Grade school children are the most vulnerable of all. The old children's verse should read like this: "Sticks and stones may break my bones, but names will never hurt me; they just bruise my heart."

If parents will follow this four-step plan, they can help their kids handle the cruel put-downs, jokes, and names that inevitably come.

Step 1—Intervene

After thirty minutes of staring in the mirror, wishing the new glasses would disappear, Ronnie approached Mom one more time.

"Mom, do I have to wear these glasses?"

"Yes! You look fine, and I know you can see better. So quit worrying about those glasses. It's time to go to school."

141

Ronnie whispered to that worried little boy in the mirror, "I don't think you look fine!"

Ronnie picked up his lunch and hurried out the door. For a moment he forgot his worry. The walk to school was filled with startling discoveries. There was a wire stretched between those poles, and now he knew how the birds were able to just sit there in the air. He really could see a lot better.

Wouldn't you know it, as soon as he walked on the school yard, Wayne, the meanest boy at school yelled, "Hey, look at Four Eyes. He's got some dumb new glasses!"

Ronnie ran as fast as he could, but not fast enough to stop the tears. He got to his first-grade classroom as the bell was ringing. As he wiped the tears from his eyes, Mrs. Smith, his teacher, told him how much she liked his new glasses. His best friend wanted to try them on. But Ronnie didn't pay any attention. That "Four Eyes" name really hurt.

At lunch Wayne was standing by the drinking fountain when Ronnie rounded the corner. Wayne yelled, "Hey, look at Four Eyes!" While Wayne was yelling, Mrs. Smith rounded the corner. She heard the harassment and called both over to her.

Ronnie was scared. He hadn't done anything.

Mrs. Smith stooped down, looked straight at Wayne and said, "Wayne, we do not make fun of people around here. That's the rule. Can you obey that rule?"

Wayne looked off in the distance and nodded yes.

"OK, go on and play," she said.

That incident didn't stop Wayne from breaking the rule, but it helped Ronnie accept the glasses. It wasn't what Mrs. Smith said, it was that she defended him and he felt special because of her action.

We must be ready to intervene in whatever way seems appropriate.

Step 2—Listen

While Mom was visiting with Grandma, Carrie ran ahead to the playground. When she arrived, her friend Heather was sitting on a bench by the swings. The boys on the swings were calling her names and proudly chanting, "Hea-ther is a dumbhead! Hea-ther is a dumbhead!"

Carrie ran up and comforted Heather from the taunts.

Later, Carrie's mother and grandma arrived. When Carrie saw her mom she grabbed Heather's hand and ran to her mom's bench. "Mom," Carrie cried, "see those boys over there? They were yelling at Heather and calling her names so I helped her."

Mom asked, "What did you help her do?"

"I helped her cry!" Carrie said as the girls walked off arm in arm.

Carrie taught her mom a great lesson that day. Later she wrote in her diary: "My first inclination would have been to defend and rescue, but after watching Heather and Carrie, I think rescue may not be as healing as sharing the hurt."

The Bible suggests a very simple formula for helping people: "Be happy with those who are happy. Be sad with those who are sad" (Romans 12:15, NCV). Empathy, feeling what your child is feeling, opens the door for healing.

Step 3—Tell about something similar happening to you

Your kids love to hear stories about when you were their age. Share how you felt when kids called you names. Tell all the details. Include what you did and what you learned.

There will be times when you will find it helpful to tell about a time when you were guilty of name calling. Sharing these stories helps empower kids to cope.

Step 4—Encourage your child to do something kind

Doing something kind for another child helps to relieve the

sting of being put down. Kindness helps get the focus off of the offended child and onto someone else. Kindness is best taught by practicing it. In fact, kindness is not kindness until it is acted out. This will be a great teaching moment to use later. So remember the details.

The amazing thing about these painful times is that doing something for another child is one of the few actions that really helps. The kindness actually takes the place of the hurt.

Allowances and Money Matters

Everyone needs an allowance. An allowance is money that can be spent any way you want. When we get to be adults, we call this our discretionary fund. Without this fund adults feel trapped.

Giving your child an allowance is a great way to begin teaching about the value of money, the difference between "wants" and "needs," and money management skills. You will find these guidelines helpful in setting the amount of allowance:

A fair allowance might be equal to the cost of a movie and snack per week. (But that doesn't mean he has to go to the movies each week.)

Some parents prorate the amounts given based on age. The weekly allowance might be $.50 for each year of age. A ten year old would get $5 weekly. Although this can be a helpful way of handling the allowance question with a number of children, it does get expensive.

Check with parents of your child's friends to see what they are doing; then do something similar.

A good time to start allowances is when your child is able to keep up with lunch money at school. Try using lunch money as a "try-out" allowance. Give the money at the first of the week, and let your child be responsible for using it correctly and for not losing the money.

When your child begins getting an allowance, he will occasionally waste his allowance on "junk." Expect it! Rather than intervening, use the natural consequence to teach a lesson.

If your child blows his money on junk, sooner or later he's bound to ask for more money to buy something important. That's your signal to say, "I really think that's something you should use your allowance for."

"But I don't have any left," comes the reply.

"Well, then, you will have to wait until next week."

Running out of money too early will usually take care of the junk problem if parents don't dole out extra cash.

It is important to realize that your young child will learn about money matters by trial and error. Don't expect perfection.

Erasing Four-Letter Words

Have you wondered where kids learn to swear and use dirty language? Ron asked several grade schoolers and got replies like these:

"I learned to swear when my dad was fixing the car."

"My friend's uncle taught him, and he taught me."

"I'm not sure."

"I learned from school, of course."

"I learned dirty words at the movies. My friend told me what the words meant, so I remembered them."

There seems to be a number of ways to deal with the dirty language and swearing problem. Here are six:

1. Ignore the word. Many kids use these inappropriate words to get attention from and shock their parents or teachers. If you sense that your child is trying out these words for attention, try not giving him what he wants.

2. Question the meaning. Say: "That's an interesting word. What does it mean? Where did you learn it?" You will get some surprising answers.

3. Use the moment for discussion. It may be that the dirty

145

word will give you the opportunity to talk about sexuality and sex education.

4. Ask your child to tell you what he's mad at. Say, "Sometimes people use words like that when they are mad at another person. If you are angry with a person, it is better to tell him you're angry."

5. Explain and set the rules. You have the right and the obligation to set the standards for language in your house. Remind the child about the rule: "No one uses words like that in this house." The message is that this kind of language is dirty and it must stop!

Eliminating Lying

Lying can become a habitual problem during elementary school years unless parents take decisive action early. Children tell lies for several reasons. Sometimes they feel like they have to make up stuff for people to listen to them. Sometimes the child is just trying to protect himself from severe punishment. For example: "All right! Who got my tools out and left them in the garage all over the floor? Whoever did it is going to get clobbered!" What would you do? Some children lie for revenge and resistance.

Lying is a signal to stop and spend some quality one-on-one time with your child. Say: "You know I love you very much, but I've been noticing something that really bothers me. And I want to talk about it. It seems to me that you have been lying a lot lately. That hurts me. The lying must stop. What can I do to help you stop?"

Remind your youngster that it will always go better for him if he tells the truth up front. He may still have to face the consequences of his actions, but lying will always make it worse.

Try these approaches for one or two weeks. Then I would urge you to get some help from a qualified therapist.

Ask your physician or minister to recommend one.

Bullies and Bandits

We are convinced that bullies and bandits simply test parents and teachers to see whether the adults are willing to take the lead and be in charge.

Granted, there are times when a pattern of aggression has been developed over time. One mother in a parents' meeting said, "I have an eight year old who is always fighting and smarting off. I can't keep my eye on him all the time. So when it gets bad, I sit on him pretty hard. It seems like the more I take charge, the more violent he gets."

The facts were that this lady and her husband got in knockdown fights all the time. We fool ourselves to think we can teach our children not to hit by hitting them.

Breaking Bad Habits

In order to help our children break bad habits, we apply the pressure. For instance:

Punishment—"Your room is a mess, so no friends can come over for a week."

Nagging—"Get ready for bed, brush your teeth, don't mess around, remember. . ."

Shaming—"You should be ashamed of a paper like that. I can't believe you turned in that kind of work."

Warning—"If you don't stop that kicking, I'll nail your shoes to the floor. Do you understand?"

Habits are not broken with comments like those. Try one of the following plans of action.

Create a new, competing habit to take the place of the old, undesirable one.

Wear out the old habit—repeat it until the child is disgusted and exhausted.

Change the setting of the habit to upset the pattern.

147

Accepting Limitations

Late one night Ron was watching one of those B-grade movies about a mad scientist. Ron can't recall the name of the movie, but the plot made a lasting impact.

The scientist and his wife were working in his laboratory late into the evening when one of the experiments back fired. The wife, who was standing closest to the experiment, was burned badly. Her face was charbroiled and became a frightening scab. The scientist kept her face covered so others would not look at her. He smashed all the mirrors as a kindness to her. He didn't think she could handle the rejection of others and the reality of her face.

The more he tried to protect her, the more she resented him. The hero of the film brings her a mirror. She takes off the bandages and looks for the first time at her mangled face. She was not pretty. In fact, her skin looked like a potato, but she survived the experience. Finally she could accept herself.

Parents have to accept themselves and their limitations. Also, we must begin to accept our children and their limitations. If we have expectations that are far beyond our limitations, then we have set ourselves up for failure and continual frustration. The challenge of parenting is to learn to accept your children as they grow and mature.

Reviewing Your Perspective

It's easy to spend all our time concentrating on problems, but that gives us an off-balance perspective of parenthood. The plan is to use the problems to teach our kids reliability, resourcefulness, and responsibility. Don't let your feelings and negative attitudes mess up your plan.

Keep your perspective on the process of helping. We are helping our kids to become responsible adults. Since we don't have a vision of the future, we are called to have faith in God. Only God can see that far ahead; that's His job. Our job is to help our kids learn how to live life right now.

CHAPTER 9
Common Sense with Sensitive Ears

11-14 years

Do You Know These Young Teens?

IT MAY SEEM LIKE YOUR YOUNGSTER has been possessed by a stranger; or you may feel you have totally lost contact. Either way, whether you know it or not, you can bet your life there is constant activity in his head. He is putting together images of what he might be, and he is going to do it by trial and error. Look for your young teen in the following descriptions. I think you will find him in or between the lines.

Ron's Story

Ron had a hunch that this wasn't going to be a good day. It was Thursday, the day Mrs. Myers, his seventh-grade counselor, would give him his class schedule. It was the fourth day of classes, and he didn't have a schedule yet. For three days he had been cooped up in the cafeteria taking placement tests.

This just wasn't fair!

"Ron? Here's your schedule!" Mrs. Myers had interrupted one of Ron's favorite daydreams, but he took the schedule, glanced at the pink paper and noticed that his first period class was English with Mr. Bell, and his second period was P.E. Fourth period was lunch. Well, at least the schedule wasn't impossible.

Finally, it was time for class, if he could just find it. With his notebook in one hand and his schedule in the other he wandered the halls till he found Room 21.

The door was closed, giving Ron time to worry awhile. A whole fist full of "what if" questions flashed through his mind. "What if they think I'm funny looking? What if they don't like my braces. What if. . . ?"

Footsteps interrupted his questions—someone was coming. Without thinking, Ron opened the door and looked in. As soon as he walked in Room 21, laughter broke out everywhere. One of the students had made a funny comment and his punch line hit at the exact moment of Ron's entry. Without knowing the facts, Ron assumed they were laughing at him. His "what if" worry had come true. This truly was one of his most embarrassing moments.

Looking for some relief, Ron walked over to the teacher. When Mr. Bell saw the pink schedule card his first words were, "Oh, no! We don't have room for any more!" Inside Ron's head those words bounced around like a racquetball, "Oh, no. . . Oh, no. . . !" There were no desks left in the room, so he sat down in the only empty chair.

While Mr. Bell went on with the class, Ron looked more closely at his schedule. "Yuk!" he said out loud. He had just noticed that he also had Mr. Bell for math and science.

Later in P.E., he had fun playing football with the guys. Ron wasn't the best in any sport, but he was better than average in all of them. And he constantly dreamed of being the best.

At lunch Ron watched the girls. The food was "garbage."

At 3:00 P.M. the bell rang, and school was over. This had been the longest day in history. As he walked down the steps of school, he thought, "It isn't fair for my grade school friends to get to go to Helms Junior High, and I have to go to this dump."

Ron had moved during the summer. His junior high school was named Edmund Downer Junior High. So far, it had truly been a downer for him.

When Ron got home Mom asked, "How was school?"

"OK," he replied.

"Did you like your teachers?"

"What teachers?"

"The ones who taught your classes."

"Which classes?"

"I don't know. Which classes do you have."

"Seventh grade classes."

"Don't get smart with me young man!"

As Ron walked away, he muttered, "There's not much chance of that at Downer!"

He went straight to his room before Mom could think of some chores for him to do. He turned on the stereo, lay down on the bed and dreamed of what Helms Junior High might have been like.

Before going to bed that night, he noticed that one of his eyes was a little lower on his face than the other. "I'm defective! No wonder those kids laughed at me today."

This was definitely not a good day.

He went to sleep worrying that all his days might turn out to be this horrible.

Keri's Story

Keri's story is told through her diary entries.

Dear Diary: I can't stand Melissa. She's a snob. Yesterday she said she was my best friend, and today

153

she forgot my name when she was introducing me to this guy. Can you believe that? Mother tried to feed us liver tonight. Yuk!! Nobody ate it, not even Dad. I hate it when it's humid. It ruins my hair. Rick called tonight. He says he hates Melissa too.

Dear Diary: Today a man spoke at church about how we should give money to relief work in Africa. I signed up to help, but only four showed up. That was really embarrassing. Our Bible class is the pits. I wouldn't say this out loud because God might be listening, but I think church is the pits too. Shock!!! I don't think I'm a spiritual person; some people aren't, you know.

Dear Diary: Tonight the whole gang did all my favorite things. Party (Yeah!). Went to the mall!!! Pizza!!! It sure beat last weekend when I had to stay home Friday and Saturday to baby-sit Jason (Yuk). I know Jason is younger than me and I should be nice to him, but he is becoming a first-class pain! I really got Melissa today. I told her, "I can't believe you're not invited to Allison's party. I thought everybody got invited." (Ha, Ha) Wow, that got her.

Dear Diary: Today was the worst day of my life. I was so embarrassed. I hate Mr. Summers. I didn't start the note, Wade did. All I did was write "OK" on the bottom of it. Then I passed it up the row, and Mr. Summers got it. He made Tom and me stand in class, and then he read the note out loud to the whole class. I hate him! It's not fair!!! And it wasn't my fault!!!!

Dear Diary: Dad has threatened to take my extension phone away. Well, that just doesn't make sense, because then I'll just be on the other phone all the time. I had a record number of phone calls yesterday—forty-seven between 3:00 P.M. and 10:00 P.M.

154

Great!!!!

Dear Diary: I got my report card today. I can't believe Mr. Perkins gave me a 77 in art. I must have missed a few assignments. I guess I was talking a little. My whole gang got kicked out of McDonald's today. The manager had the nerve to accuse us of being too loud. We were just having fun. (Ha, Ha)

Dear Diary: Today my new favorite color is red. My favorite flavor of ice cream is "Cookies 'n Cream." And, I have a new favorite radio station. There may be something wrong with me. I seem to be changing a lot lately. Mom says I'm going crazy. Wrong!!!!!!

Dear Diary: I think my mom is out to get me. She is on the warpath about my room. It's exactly like I want it. She called it a pigpen, I mean really! I think Mom just doesn't understand how different things are today. After all, she's been an adult forever.

Dear Diary: I found Kevin's locker today. I walked by it twelve times. Allison was with me when we saw him. I told her not to look at him, and she looked. I was soooooooo embarrassed!!! He is soooooooo cute. I told Mom I was in love—I'll never tell her that again. She said that I'm not old enough to know what love is. I don't think my mother has ever been in love like I am.

What's Behind the Face?

Did you meet your boy or girl in the descriptions of Ron and Keri? With all the pressures on the outside, it's hard to really get in touch with what's going on inside.

It was Saturday at lunch, and Ron was sitting in a popular restaurant observing people. Two tables to my left was a fine-looking father-and-son team. The man was in his thirties, and the boy, I learned later, was eleven. Both wore Polo shirts,

Docker pants and the latest in fashionable running shoes. They looked alike, dressed alike and thought alike.

After the waitress brought their drinks, the boy put his chin on his hands and his elbows on the table. He looked straight at his dad and said, "I'm depressed, Dad!"

Dad responded, "I know; so am I."

They continued to talk as Ron left the restaurant. This boredom syndrome is a result of the pressure we put our kids under to be "mini" adults. We push them to grow up far before they're ready. It seems to me that childhood is vanishing before our eyes as we watch it.

There is a scene in *Zorba the Greek* where Zorba watches a butterfly trying to break free of its cocoon. The struggle seemed too intense, so, with good intentions, Zorba bent down and breathed his warm, moist breath on the butterfly. His breath released the butterfly. It was free, but its wings were not strong enough yet. The freed butterfly fought for several minutes and then died.

When a young teen is hurried and pressured to be an adult, he is like that butterfly. He is freed too early from childhood, and he launches too soon into adulthood. The stress of the transition forces him to become extremely self-focused and fearful of failure. This self-focus makes it difficult to be aware of the feelings and needs of others. Literally, this pressured teen becomes the center of his own universe.

He is expected to dress, act and think like an adult, so he play-acts. He pretends. However, unlike the butterfly, he carries his cocoon around with him and occasionally slips back into the old familiar childish behavior.

Let us vow to reduce this pressure on our kids. Let us promise that we will not push our children to grow up before their time.

Putting the Pieces Together

The young teen is constantly trying to put together his own puzzle of life. Just about the time he has one part together, he discovers he can't find the pieces for the other part. Trying to put a puzzle together when you can't locate all the pieces is pretty frustrating.

Add to this frustration a genetic clock that winds each young teen up differently, and you have an unusual picture. I like to compare the young teenager to a juggler on a high wire who is trying to keep balanced and juggle all the balls in the air at the same time while his hands sometimes go on strike and stop listening to his head. It could be a mess. It's a challenge undoubtedly, but with some common sense, it can be an action-packed adventure thriller with just enough danger to be really exciting.

Chart 5 suggests that during the young teen years parents should be gradually releasing the decision-making process to the kids. Catching them doing it right and using logical consequences are extremely effective with these ages. In order to

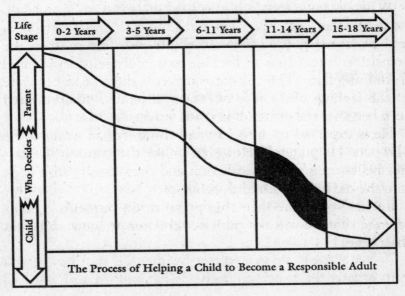

Life Stage	0-2 Years	3-5 Years	6-11 Years	11-14 Years	15-18 Years

Who Decides — Parent — Child

The Process of Helping a Child to Become a Responsible Adult become responsible, the young teen must have opportunities to learn by facing the consequences of his behavior. Don't spend your time rescuing him.

Many parents greet the teenage years with dread. They have heard the war stories and they're afraid. Ron advises that those parents who expect teenage rebellion may actually foment an uprising. Although many experts of the 1970s warned about the rebellious tendencies of the teenage years, we have since discovered those warnings were based on studies of teens who had already rebelled, big time. Average teens are just not bent toward rebellion, a little banter maybe, but not rebellion. We have good kids, and we would do well to expect the best, not the worst.

One of the most important characteristics of a great parent during these stressful years is a sense of humor. A sense of humor helps us keep things in perspective. Parents who can see the difference between the important issues and trivial ones will be able to guide their children through these years with far less pain than they ever expected possible.

The Nine Most Repeated Sayings

It's Not Fair!"

This saying needs a little interpreting. When your early teen complains that he is not being treated fairly, set up a time to have a discussion about the situation. Depending on the problem at hand, make several overdrawn, unreasonable statements like:

"You can't get any new shoes because your sister's shoes are still in good shape, and I want to treat you two equally."

"Since I'm feeling ill and will have to stay home, I expect you to stay home too."

"If you want to be treated equally, then I'll start buying you both exactly the same size clothes. That will make it easier to shop."

Even if they never admit it, most teens will get the point. Since it's obvious they don't want to be treated equally, then you can tell them that you will do your best to treat them fairly. Fairly means you will take into account their own individual needs, differences and wants.

Let them know that whenever they feel like they are being treated unfairly, you will be willing to listen to their viewpoint so long as they are willing to listen to yours. That's fair.

Cheating

With all the pressure to perform and achieve these days, it's no wonder that young teens are cheating to make grades. Interviews with students indicate that forty-five to fifty percent of young teens cheat occasionally.

Kathy says she cheats, only a little. "You have to. The teacher grades on a curve, and about ten to twelve kids in the class cheat—they blow the curve. I've got to cheat to stay up with the class."

Skip decided not to cheat, "I've had the chance several times to study the actual test I would take the next day, and I turned it down. I'd hate the way I'd feel afterwards."

Holly added, "I don't cheat, but ratting on the kids that do is worse than cheating. It's no big deal."

The decision to cheat or not to cheat is one of personal conviction plus courage. Most of our young teens have the conviction. What some of them lack is the courage to act on conviction. In family conferences across America Ron has taught that the crucial issue is courage. And a renewed priority placed on the shaping of Christian character is long overdue. Invite a small group of young teens over for pizza and interview them about courage. Ask questions like, "Tell about someone you know who demonstrates courage. How do you know if you have courage? When is it tough to be courageous? How do people learn to be courageous? How can adults help teenagers to have the courage to stand up for their convictions?" Your job in the interview is just to ask questions and listen—nothing else.

Cleaning

You may find it difficult to believe, but several different surveys reveal that sixty-five to seventy-five percent of young teens feel they should be responsible for straightening and cleaning their own rooms. In addition to their own rooms, these kids should also help around the house with the regular chores. It should be that way because they are still members of the family, even though you might wonder about that at times.

It will be helpful to have a one-on-one discussion about how clean is "clean." Their room is fast becoming their private world, and to challenge their world is like challenging them. Come to some kind of compromise that works for both of you. Pray for tolerance.

Moving

Moving your young teen at this sensitive time can be traumatic. She will feel "jerked up" from friends, school, church, and her favorite mall. One or more of the following suggestions will help.

Take your teenager with you when you look for your new home. Ask for her input in the selection.

Have your young teen gather information about the city: schools, churches, places of special interest, recreational parks, etc.

Find a teen about your teen's age to be a friend and show her the ropes.

Emphasize the new start and how great it's going to be, but be willing to talk about the memories of the old place and how good it was.

Encourage your teen to write friends in the old town and to keep in touch with what's happening.

"Why Can't I . . .

. . . do what I want?"

You can help your young teen learn responsibility by:

Asking him to write a one-page proposal describing the reasons for and against doing what he wants.

Trading sides in the discussion. You take your kid's side and ask him to take your side.

Realizing that he may be just testing your resolve to be the leader of the family. He has developed new debate skills, and this is a great time to use them.

Discussing the feelings on both sides. Listen and work out alternatives if necessary, but never argue about feelings.

. . . go where I want?"

It will help your young teen to discuss the following:

Ask your teen to suggest five reasons why he should get to go where he wants. You suggest five also. Then discuss why it's important to limit where a young teen may go.

Set up some limits so that your teen knows ahead of time what places are off-limits.

If you have personal experiences that relate to where your teen wants to go, share your story.

. . . talk like I want?"

Sarcastic and critical talk is tough to deal with. Try some of these methods:

Helping them to find something to do that they are good at will build their self-confidence, thus removing the motivation for being so critical. Although they are critical of others, they are most critical of themselves.

Placing a moratorium on sarcastic talk for everyone in your family. Anyone who is critical or sarcastic has to go to time-out for five minutes.

Demanding a verbal apology for each sassy remark. You may not change their thinking, but you can put some limits on their talk.

Doing away with all forms of put-down and sarcastic humor by anyone in your family.

"How Embarrassing!"
Keri and Her Body

When young teens are asked if they would like to change anything about their bodies, they almost always respond, "Yes!" Keri is concerned about her body. In P.E. when they have to take showers, Keri runs through the shower but hardly gets wet because she is embarrassed about her body. It seems like she's the only girl who really doesn't need a bra.

She was glad that her mother took the time to explain to her about periods and what to expect, but having her period at school is a constant source of embarrassment. She understands why some of the girls call it "The Curse."

Keri is a Christian and wants to dress modestly. Because of her convictions, there are times at the beach when she is embarrassed, but she is curious at the same time. Every once in a while, one of the gang will have a "sex" magazine. She can hardly believe what she sees on the pages. Keri's not even sure that Mom and Dad still "have sex." The whole subject is embarrassing to talk about with anyone except her close friends, so when some adult brings it up, the natural thing to do is giggle.

Keri may never ask her mom or her dad about anything related to sex. Her parents need to know what she is thinking about and what embarrasses her and what questions she has. One way to start the discussion is for one of the parents to spend some time talking about what the concerns were when he/she was a kid. These talks should be often, casual and short.

Kevin and His Body

Kevin's head is filled with concern about his body. Like Keri, he is totally embarrassed by the showers at school. He isn't nearly as developed as some of the other boys. There are times when he will spend hours wondering whether his penis will ever get to the right size or if he is defective.

During these early years of sexual development, many boys have strange fantasies about all kinds of sexual behavior. Because of these fantasies, a few boys grow up thinking they are sexually "different." Some will spend years secretly thinking that they must be homosexual because that's the only explanation they can come up with.

The first time Kevin had a wet dream he spent a week feeling guilty. Nobody had talked to him about it, and he sure wasn't going to talk to Mom or Dad. That would be total embarrassment.

While he was working on math problems at the end of math class he suddenly noticed that he had an erection. The bell rang; he put his math book in front of himself and walked out of the room. That whole day he wondered if he was "oversexed" or something.

Every time Kevin masturbates he feels guilty and evil. He has never heard anyone at church talk about it, so he doesn't know what to think.

Kevin needs to talk to someone other than his peers. Most of his embarrassment is due to lack of information. For example, fears about being homosexual are fairly common today. Just because someone has weird fantasies doesn't mean he is gay.

Wet dreams are a little disturbing at first, but they are natural, neither right nor wrong. Kevin's erection is called a spontaneous erection and most boys experience them, though not always in math class. Masturbation is practiced today by ninety percent of young teen boys and fifty percent of young teen girls. The Bible doesn't say anything about the subject, but it does talk about how problems we face can take control of us. Masturbation can become a habit that controls a youngster early on in life.

Spend some time talking informally about your sexual struggles as a young teenager. Take regular times to talk about some of these embarrassing concerns; your teen will be glad you did, even if he never tells you so.

"I Don't Have Anything to Wear!"
Fashion and Fads

Kids will always have fads and fashions unique to their culture. Some will be humorous, and some will be stupid. Others will take kids to the edge of acceptance by society. Often kids begin to take on the personality of the fad. When they try on more than the clothes, then it's time to discuss it, change it, or stop it.

One of the most difficult tasks a parent has is helping a young teenager become accepted in the group. Try some of the following ideas:

Do some research. Find another loner who doesn't seem to fit in. Get the two together and see what happens. Remember, don't try to force friendship. The end result of force is resentment.

Discuss friendship and the need for friends with your teen. Tell your teen that God can use our alone times to prepare us for some great service. Ask, "What do you think He is preparing you for?"

Plan trips with families with similar-aged children.

Realize as a parent that you can't make friends for them. Let them experience the consequences of the alone time, and God will bless it. If, however, the teen seems to go into a depressed state beyond moodiness, then get some immediate counseling help.

"It Wasn't My Fault!"
Blaming Others

Ron meets people every day who seem to be eager to blame their failure or their condition on their past, their parents, their boss, or their God. According to *Denver Post* columnist Woody Paige, back in the late 1980s a schoolteacher originally raised the issue. She said,

> I'm tired of students always having an excuse for everything. Nothing's ever their fault. Used to be when one of my students didn't get his homework turned in, I'd ask why and he'd say, "Well, I fell asleep and I didn't do it." Now it's because the electricity went out on their house or they developed some sudden paralysis in their right hand that went away the next morning. Or "I did my homework and we have a poltergeist in our attic and just as I was about to fall asleep, the poltergeist forced me into the time warp into another dimension and there I was attacked by 3,000 ghosts and goblins and I died. I was brought back to life by the good fairy, and I was able to escape back to the room. As I reentered the atmosphere, there was an explosion which consumed my homework in flames."

Where do kids get such wild stories? Paige writes, "They get them from adults." He tells of Rob Williams, a one-time Denver Nugget player in the NBA, who had a rather nasty habit of occasionally not showing up for games. And he always had an excuse.

According to Williams, his apartment was robbed 38 times, he was involved in 47 automobile accidents, 6 grandmothers died, he was kidnapped and left in the mountains 12 times, and he had 4 flat tires once after being bit by a poisonous rattlesnake. Now, Williams is no longer in the NBA. Whose fault is that? Certainly not Williams's.

Try doing an "excuses analysis" this week. Keep a record of the number of times you make excuses during the next seven days. Then do whatever is necessary to reduce that number by at least twenty percent per week. You will be surprised what a change you will see in your children.

Coping with Failure

Forgiveness is the key to coping with failure. Before a teen can pick up the pieces and learn from a failure, he must experience forgiveness. Parents can help a young teen feel forgiven only if *they* are willing to forgive.

However, if a child is to cope with failure, he must also face the consequences of the failure. Don't rob your teen of the consequences of his failure. When your young teen has damaged personal property, he should be responsible for fixing or replacing that property. Doesn't that make sense?

Fighting with Friends/Siblings

Some fights are Trivial Fights:

"You're on my side!"

"She's breathing my air!"

"He hit me!"

Teens turn these arguments on and off. At times they argue because they're hungry, tired, bored or confused. It's almost impossible to discover who started it or why it began.

Just stay cool; the kids really love each other.

A few fights are Topic Fights:

"Butter is not good for you!"

"My friend said so!" "Well, then she's wrong!"

It doesn't take long for the kids to realize that they will have differences of opinion—that's OK. This kind of arguments becomes a verbal debate.

Some fights are Attack Fights:

"Give that back, you turkey!"

"I said, get out of my room!"

"You jerk, stay out of my life!"

These fights can lead to hitting, kicking, and biting. For sure, these fights result in name calling and put-downs. Attack fights are harmful to the kids and destructive to the family atmosphere, so this kind of fight should be eliminated.

Parents can help by:

Understanding why. The whys are like symptoms of something not being quite right. Parents could demand the fighting stop, but the cause may continue inside and undetected.

Developing a positive home atmosphere. A positive home encourages positive feelings in all the family members. If the teens feel good about themselves they will be more likely to feel good about others.

Helping the kids learn to express anger constructively.

Jason and Cliff were yelling about Jason's records. They began calling each other names and throwing things in the room. Parents tend to use one of the following tactics in coping with this situation:

Leaving them alone. Let them fight it out. Of course this doesn't teach them much about getting along.

"You guys have three minutes to solve your problem, or you'll be grounded for the weekend." They will probably comply, but the real frustration is still there.

Assuming the oldest is responsible. "Jason, I'm ashamed of you. You're the oldest; can't you act a little older?" Here the oldest learns that he gets blamed for everything. The youngest learns he can get away with anything.

Try this: "OK! Calm down. Jason, you look pretty upset. Let's work this out. What are you angry about? Tell me how you feel. Cliff, tell me your side, How do you feel? Jason would you feel better about this if. . ." This models a constructive way to handle anger.

"I'm Not a Kid Anymore!"
Deciding about Drugs and Alcohol

The following six steps will help keep young teens free of drugs and alcohol:

1. Get the facts. The drugs kids are taking today are more potent, more dangerous, and more addictive than ever in history. Know the symptoms of drug abuse:

chronic dishonesty
increasing and inappropriate anger
reduced motivation
diminished interest in activities
downward turn in grades
memory lapses
bloodshot eyes
hostility in discussing drugs
wide mood swings

2. Build family loyalty. Begin or revive traditions that help kids see your family as special and unique. One family made a "Family Commercial," describing why a person might want to be a member of their family. They used a video camera, interviews, and drama. Sure, it was a little embarrassing, but the kids have never forgotten it. A friend of mine told of a dad who spends one Saturday a quarter taking the family on all day photo-rallies. The pictures turn out great. The memories are still developing

3. Give each child a blessing. Low self-esteem is a common denominator in all drug-abuse problems. Here's where parents can make a big difference with what seems like little things.

Introduce them to your adult friends and claim the kids, publicly. Hug them regularly, whether they need it or not.

Establish a "no put-down" policy that includes jokes, and never embarrass your kids in front of friends or enemies.

Listen to your young teen's dreams and tell them about yours back in the "old days."

4. Teach children how to make their own decisions. This is natural turf for many of us.

Help them think of alternative solutions and write them down. Ask the "What would happen if" questions. Tell about your decisions.

5. Encourage their spiritual side. Research indicates that religious commitment and resistance to drug abuse are connected. Take your kid to church—just going to church helps.

6. Parents must constantly re-evaluate their own behavior. I promise you, your kids already have. Courageous families can win this war.

Deciding about Tobacco

In several states the rage among boys 11-15 years old is trying smokeless tobacco. It seems that about half the young teens are trying "dip," the stuff you put between your lower lip and gums. Somehow they think this stuff is safer. It's not.

Tobacco is still a messy problem. It has been proven to cause cancer, yet we continue to feed the habit. If your teen is using tobacco in any form, sit down and calmly discuss the problems you have with it. Discuss an appropriate plan for stopping the habit. It may take some pretty strong consequences to get the tobacco use stopped, but it must be done. The restriction of stereo, phone, and TV privileges is usually effective.

Deciding about Sex

When there is pressure to be sexually active during these early years, a teenager has five choices. Which one would your teen choose?

Give in.

Say no because they're scared.

Run.

Say no because this is not the right time.

Thank God for the gift of sex, but keep it under wraps.

I know of at least eight reasons why your young teen should not be sexually active. You will undoubtedly think of others. Use this as a resource for writing a letter to your teen or for having a talk with your teen (or both).

1. Being sexually active before marriage makes sex less special and sets you up to lose some of the potential ecstasy of sex.

2. If you get involved sexually with the person you are dating, sex takes over the relationship—it always happens that way if the relationship survives sex.

3. If you decide to be sexually active you will have to do something with the guilt. If it's not handled it will cause sexual problems later on. Guilt by itself is powerful enough to cause major problems with sex in the future.

4. Sex for pleasure outside the bounds of marriage plants the seeds of loneliness. And some say it can turn sex into an addictive behavior.

5. Sex before marriage distracts from the key word used to describe marriage in the Bible—fidelity!

6. Sex before marriage actually breaks up more relationships than it strengthens.

7. Sex drives in the teen years need to be controlled because your emotions mature more slowly than your body. Just because the sex drive works doesn't mean you are ready to use it.

8. It is very easy to mix up your desires. You may really want affection and think that sex is the only way to get it. If you get healthy amounts of affection, you may find less problems controlling your sexual desires.

Deciding about Faith

Parents can shape their teen's faith by doing these seven things:

1. Take your teen to church. The Sunday services, Bible classes, youth devotionals, special events, camps, and other church times play a vital role in helping to shape faith.

2. Your teen needs to be around "faith" people—people who trust God for their future. Teens need to hear these people tell about what God is doing in their lives.

3. Start where they are. Accept them right there, pimples and all, doubts and all.

4. Use the everyday moments to talk about God and His directing of your life. Problems, crises, routines, and celebrations all fit together as a tapestry of learning events. Take advantage of the moments.

5. Help your teen get to know God. Encourage your teen to have a personal study time. Talk about God in personal terms and study the Bible as if you were learning more and more about a best friend. Spend special times praying with your youngster.

6. Look for the supernatural. Faith is seeing something that isn't there yet. If we are looking, God is still in the supernatural business.

7. Tell your story. Make sure your teen knows how you came to the Lord, what kind of struggles you've had, and what kind of victories you've received.

"You Don't Understand!"
Going Together

Most young teens don't talk to their parents about romantic things. They are very serious when they say, "You don't understand." In fact, teens doubt that anyone feels what they feel. It would not be unheard of for a young teen to say, "You don't know what love is; you have never loved like I love!" Have patience and accept their biased view with grace.

Breaking Up

A breakup is like an emotional amputation. You can help your teen cope with the loss:

Accept it as painful, real and over.

Help him talk about the pain. Pain is a sign of healing. It is absolutely essential to feel it and talk about it.

Get your teen back with friends. Encourage him to go with a same sex friend to work out or participate in some other physical activity.

Tell him he'll know that the relationship is finished when he can walk past that person in the hall and say "Hi" without it bringing up all the hurt. Reassure him that it is possible. Get your teen doing something for someone else. Giving him responsibilities will take his mind off the rejection.

Silence

There are times when teens want their parents out of their hair. Under normal circumstances, let their silence be. Don't expect your young teen to talk with you about all the things he talked about as a child. It is important to note, however, that silence is one of the first warning signs of depression.

Distrust

Three turtles decided to go to the beach for a picnic. One was to bring the food, another the drinks, and the third turtle was to carry the umbrella. They got about halfway there when the turtle who was supposed to have the drinks discovered that he had forgotten the ice chest. One of his buddies suggested that the forgetful turtle should go back and get the drinks, and the other two would wait there.

"No, you'll go on without me!"

"No, we won't. You go on! We'll wait right here."

So the forgetful turtle left, and the two buddies rested by a big rock. They waited two days. . . three days. . . and on the fourth day one of them turned to the other and suggested, "Well, I think we'd better go on. I don't think he's coming back."

Just then out from behind a rock came the forgetful turtle crying out, "I knew you wouldn't wait. I knew it! I knew it!"

During these early teen years your teen is a lot like a turtle.

At times he will stick his neck out and make a lot of progress, at other times he will pull inside his shell and hide away. Either way, his peers have conditioned him to be distrustful of adults in general and parents specifically. So if you have the distrustful turtle living with you, shoot straight with him. Don't give him simple answers to complex questions. Talk it out; honesty is the only way to counteract distrust.

Almost Grown

Living with young teenagers is a challenging experience. Every part of life is lived with intensity. When they are down, they're really down, and when they're up, they're flying. Don't push them into adulthood before their time.

Listen to them speak. There is a hidden message behind every word. Give them the chance to make their own decisions about important things. Expect some failure and some pain. Let them learn from their mess-ups; don't spend your time rescuing them.

And, look for ways to open discussion and build trust.

How to Talk to Your Teen about Virginity

As kids grow older they really do want to talk to their parents about the struggles they face. But if you wait for your kids to ask you, you may wait a lifetime. After a seminar held on the campus of a prominent Christian university a young lady pulled Ron aside and said, "Let me tell you what my dad did. When I was in the seventh grade he took me out to dinner. It was real special. He said, 'Amy, what I'm about to tell you is very important. I want to share with you some secrets about boys. I want you to know how to hold on to your principles when you get with a boy who's lost his.'"

She continued, "We talked for the rest of the evening. Don't you think I'm lucky to have a father like that?" Yes, I do.

What would you say if your daughter, or your son for that matter, asked, "How far can I go and be safe," or "Where should I draw the line," or "If I don't want to get totally involved, what can I do to keep my cool?" These are the real-life questions. Do you have real life answers? My problem is one of context. I want to set the stage, explain the philosophy and explain the reasons. Our kids want simple, uncomplicated answers.

Here's what I say. "If you stay above the neck, you're safe. Below the neck can get you in trouble. I would have to be a block of ice to tell you never to kiss or be affectionate. If you like each other, you will want to be close. So the question is where to draw the line?" The answer is, "Keep hands outside each other's clothes. The minute you get your hands inside each other's clothes, you're headed for big trouble. Skin touching skin below the neck turns on things you may not be able to control right now. Passion is like money: you always want more. What you do one night won't be enough for the next night. Someday you'll thank God that He's made you with all this passion. But until that day you need to draw a line and stick with it, no matter what."

Can you speak that way to your daughter, to your son? I hope you can. Our kids need all the help they can get, and they want the help to come from us. If you anticipate trouble talking this way to your kids, write your counsel in a letter and send it through the mail. I guarantee they will read the letter. No one has more influence in this area of your child's life than you do.

CHAPTER 10
Put the Monkey on Their Back

15-18 Years

HIGH SCHOOLERS REMIND ME OF SATELLITES. They are very expensive to launch. Each day is spent circling just out of reach of the launch area. Invariably, the communications link fouls up, or there is a malfunction and the circuits go haywire. If communication actually stops, it must be due to some sort of electrical interference.

Satellites are connected with ground control and yet are independent of the Earth's environment. It has taken years of development to prepare them for their destiny—to fly freely, but with a purpose.

After years of testing, teenagers should be ready for the freedom to fly, make mistakes and find their purpose while still living within the limitations of their home. To do this they need to be given guided independence and growing responsibility. They need to feel the joy of impending adulthood and the load of personal responsibility. In short they need to live with the monkey on *their* back for a while, not their parent's back.

Keeping the monkey on the teenager's back helps him to develop independence, learn to cope with his anxieties, and discover how to manage conflict. Remember, it is the goal of common sense discipline to help parents raise children who have learned how to take charge of their own lives. You will find structure and limitations are still needed, although the most reliable structure now will be your teen's own conscience. Setting the limits is still your job. Rules and limits are like old friends, comforting to have around, and always there if you need them. And you will still need them.

Who's In Charge

In order for a teenager to be in charge of his own life, he must know what to do with at least three monkeys.

1. The Monkey of Independence—This means responsibility must shift from the parent to the teen. It's time to practice living with more freedoms. These freedoms do prove to be more difficult to live with than we have anticipated.

2. The Monkey of Anxiety—This means the teen must know what to do with his worries and emotional concerns. No one can do another person's worrying for him, but through the years parents have sure tried.

3. The Monkey of Conflict—This means the teen must know appropriate ways to work out differences and make adjustments. Some adults still don't know how to do that.

Chart 6 recommends that most of the decisions during these later years be made by the teen. Putting the monkey on his back will force him to take responsibility for his successes and face the consequences of his failures. You will still find it necessary to place limits on activities and determine appropriate consequences. Don't forget to look for things he is doing right. Expecting the best in your teen will help him develop

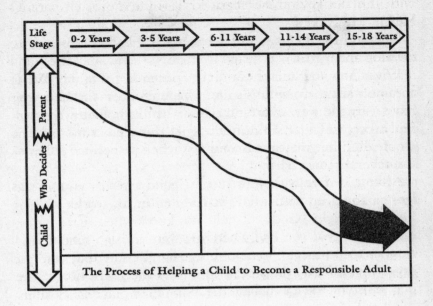

Life Stage	0-2 Years	3-5 Years	6-11 Years	11-14 Years	15-18 Years

The Process of Helping a Child to Become a Responsible Adult

an "I can" attitude toward conquering any tough problem.

Developing Independence

Setting Goals

You can help your teenager become more independent by encouraging him to set his own goals and then giving him the freedom to work toward those goals.

Leo Randolph had what many people would call an unrealistic goal. For years he had trained to be the best. Leo wanted to win a gold medal in the 1976 Olympics. The experts didn't give Leo a chance. He was only eighteen years old, and he had no experience at the international level.

But Leo had an undeniable drive to achieve the gold. He had a poster-size picture taken of himself with a gold medal around his neck. That poster was positioned so that every morning when Leo opened his eyes the first thing he saw was

Leo with the gold and a caption, "Leo Randolph Wins Gold Medal." It worked.

Leo won the 112-pound boxing class! He had motivation, training and a goal.

What does your teen have on the poster in his mind? What does he want to do with his life? What choices is he thinking about? By the way, in an interview with his hometown newspaper, Leo said that winning the gold was a great moment in his life, but the greatest moment was when he became a Christian several years earlier.

Arrange a date with your teen. Spend the first part of the date catching up with what's happening in his world. When the time is right (God will help you know when, if you ask), tell about a goal you had when you were in high school, and ask your teen to share some of his goals. Be sure that you just listen. Even if you disagree with one of the goals, now is the time to listen. You can debate the morality or practicality later.

Priority or Privacy

When it comes to privacy, some parents are uncomfortable putting the monkey on the teenager's back. During adolescence teens are very sensitive about their privacy needs; also parents are very suspicious about what goes on in private. Ron believe some teens deliberately leave their rooms a mess because they think that will keep Mom out. They will pay the price of the hassle if they can keep Mom out, thus having their privacy.

The Bedroom

One of Ron's best friends has a teenage daughter. She has a typical problem with her room. Let me describe it: Posters overlap to completely cover one wall of Abby's room. Fingernail polish, old movie tickets, ribbons from the pep rally, notes from friends, records, discarded makeup, and a bag of corn chips are stacked and scattered over the desktop. Hanging on the closet door are three sets of clothes she tried on this morning before deciding what to wear. The stereo is playing the same CD over and over. Pillows and stuffed animals are stacked on top of the bed. Her mirror is edged with notes from Danny. Danny's autographed picture is stuck at lip level on the mirror. Somewhere among the animals, clothes and CD cases is a telephone—her daily lifeline to the world.

This is the place where Abby talks, studies, plans, thinks, dreams, prays, and cries. It's her private world. She considers her room to be as private as her mail, her phone calls, and her diary. And she feels she ought to be free to keep her room just the way she wants.

While we were there recently Ron overheard, "Abby Elaine Thomason, you get in here right now and get this room of yours straightened, before company comes, or you can consider yourself grounded for the weekend!"

Embarrassed, Abby ran back down the hall. Her privacy had been challenged, so she defended herself, "My room is just like I like it!"

"I've told you before what I think of your back talk, young lady. You're grounded for this weekend, and if you say another word you're grounded for a month!" Mom was livid.

Abby slammed her door, turned up the stereo, and, I'm sure, carried on a conversation with herself, defending herself. Then, she got on the phone to see what was happening. Then, as though it were a badge of honor, she told all the memorable details of the skirmish. During that phone call you can bet she said, "I can't wait to get out of this house where I can be on my own!"

At the beginning of this conflict a slight change of words might have avoided the ensuing battle.

"Abby, we've got company, and I'm in a real time squeeze. I know they won't be in your room, but would you at least pick

179

up the big chunks? It doesn't have to pass inspection, but I would sure feel more at ease."

This way the issue stays centered on the room cleaning and "how clean is clean" and not on a developing power struggle between Mom and Abby. In order for Mom to feel comfortable making these changes, she must be able to accept the fact that Abby might like her private world a little more cluttered than Mom does.

Abby must realize that her room is connected to the other rooms in the house and should meet the same general standards as the rest of the house. If she does not respond by keeping up to those standards then some appropriate consequences are in order.

Limited use of "family" property like the car or phone might be of help.

Accepting Personal Likes

Another monkey with which parents have difficulty is coping with personal likes and dislikes of their teenagers. There are three hallmarks of independence that parents in every generation have trouble accepting:

Fashion—You may have noticed that in the push for separation from their parents' culture, teenagers won't be caught dead wearing something that's not accepted by their culture. The "geeks" would stay home before they would dress in the fashion of the "preps."

Music—Ron has divided teens into groups by asking what radio stations they listen to most often. There is security in knowing everyone likes your favorite music. In many ways the Top Ten songs help some teens decide what they are supposed to like. So, generally with music, independence is measured by how different it is from old fogy's music.

Friends—Sometimes our own flesh and blood will pick the most unusual characters as friends. You may find you don't

know why you dislike this latest friend, or you may know
exactly:
clothes
breath
hair
language
laughter
none of the above
all of the above
You may have a socially conscious teen who is seriously trying to touch human need. Or your teen may be eagerly trying
to be evangelistic with God's message of grace. ·

Even though you want to honor the independence of your
teen, you have not abdicated your place as parent. You still
have an obligation to intervene when you suspect personal
welfare is at stake. In fact there will be times when you have
to intervene. Intervening means you impose preset family
rules concerning behavior or speech. For example:

"No one in this family buys or plays music that has degrad-
ing, profane, or erotic lyrics. Those records must go!"

"All members of this family are free to choose their own
clothes as long as they are decent and will not embarrass the
rest of us!"

"In this family we select our friends from people who share
our beliefs about God and the Christian lifestyle."

When a teen's personal preferences violate the values of
your family, try this discussion:

"You know I love you and I always will. I want you to know
how proud I am of you and the way you are growing up. But I
am concerned about your friend, Richard. Can we talk about
him? He looks like a doper to me; is he?"

"If he is a doper, let's find some way to help him, if he wants
help. Ask him over and let's both talk with him. If he refuses
help, then I believe you need to break off the friendship.

What do you think?"

Sometimes you discover personal preferences long after they have been adopted. Dealing with a tape collection of lewd and erotic music, one parent tried this:

"Craig, I just happened to listen to the words of that tape you had on last night. Are you aware of the words? They are just not acceptable in this house. Let's talk about what we can do about this."

"I don't want to censor everything you listen to, and I won't, but I believe that tape should be destroyed. I'll tell you what. If you'll destroy the tape, I will give you enough money to replace it with one with acceptable lyrics. Deal? By the way, I really like this other tape. What do you think about it?"

When you find yourself in a situation that has your teen tied into a complicated, unhealthy web of relationships and absolutely nothing seems to work, I recommend looking at the option of moving. Though there are enormous financial burdens, I do know a number of families who have made move decisions because of harmful or toxic relationships, and God has blessed them greatly. In the new environment the teen has a chance to establish a new identity, free of the negative influences.

Asking questions and listening, regardless of the answers, will help you do the best thing for your teen. So many parents don't listen. Parents who don't listen build a wall of resentment in their teen's heart.

Questions help the teen to search his own mind and to think about the answers (even if he gives you a glib response at the time). Listening beyond the words builds respect.

Sometimes compromises are necessary, and at times parents should accept differences in personal preference without comment.

This strategy may destroy the motivation for the questionable behavior in the first place. (Shaking up the parent may have been the goal).

Freedom and the Automobile

For the typical high school kid in America, getting a driver's license is a rite of passage to independence—"At last I am free!" Ron asked a perceptive sixteen-year-old boy, "What's so great about having your own car?"

He replied,

> Having a car is better than having a room of your own. In a car you are free, you can get away from the house. I feel grown up just riding around with a friend—as long as there is no adult in the car. While you're driving you can play the stereo as loud as you want and nobody yells at you.
>
> Having a car makes me feel like a man. Sometimes I like to show off a little. Don't tell my dad that—I'll have to pay for the tires. Cuttin' up a little shows everybody that I'm in control. Nobody is telling me what to do. I am making the decisions; I have the power. I think that's why girls are always interested in your car.
>
> There's something thrilling about the risk of driving fast on a mountain road or seeing how fast the old clunker will go. My car is more than just a set of wheels. It's kinda like a part of my body.

Listen carefully to the words of this boy. He is telling you something that might jog your memory of days long gone by. Your high schooler will probably never tell you these things. Assuming them to be true will help you understand what's happening as your teen begins a love affair with his car.

Trust Your Teenager as a Driver

Spend time riding in the car while your teen is driving. The more you know of his skills, the more you will trust him.

Conduct regular maintenance checks on the cars your family owns. Everyone should know the basics about the car—like the difference between the radiator and the carburetor.

Develop a list of safety rules for your whole family.

Talk openly about driving experiences. Share your mess-ups and encourage your teen to share his.

If your teen has a car of his own, he should be responsible for its upkeep, its operation and at least a portion of its cost.

Realize trust is a decision, not a feeling. It takes time to let our feelings catch up with your decision, so be patient.

An automobile is a challenge to any teenager's self-control. If he knows you are aware of how much the car means to him and you are flexible where you can be, your teen will be too. He will be as self-controlled in the car as you are.

Drinking and Driving

According to the National Highway Safety Administration, arrests of teens for drunk driving have more than tripled since 1960, and accidents are the leading cause of death for fifteen to twenty-four year olds in America. Of course, you know we have a problem with teenage drinking and driving because you pay the insurance premiums.

Driving demands alertness and self-control, so use words like these for your teen: "I don't want you riding in a car if I don't know the driver. If I've never met the driver, please introduce us. You know me well enough to know that if the driver ever appears stoned or drunk or goofy (more than the usual teenager), you'll have to get another ride or stay home. While we're on the subject, anytime a driver of a car you're in starts to drink, ask if you can get out as soon as possible. Call me, and I'll come get you. If you ever drink while you're the driver, do not under any circumstance drive. Call me, and I'll come and get you! No hassles till the next day. I know I can depend on you to drive safely."

Making Decisions on Their Own

The best way to help your teenager make decisions for himself is to keep the monkey on his back. Give him situations where he has to decide, where he has the opportunity to fail. The Bible puts it this way: "It is good for a man to bear the yoke while he is young. Let him sit alone in silence, for the Lord has laid it on him. Let him bury his face in the dust—there may yet be hope" (Lamentations 3:27-29).

Ron knows some teenagers who don't make any decisions concerning their lives. They just go along with whom ever they're with. If it feels OK, do it. By high school teens should be making most of their decisions for themselves. Here's how to help your kid do just that.

Checklist for Helping Teens Make Decisions

Every decision can be evaluated on the basis of two dimensions:

1. Quality—Is it important that the decision be right, true to values and beliefs—the best choice?

2. Acceptance—Is it important that the decision be accepted by others?

For example, after a youth gathering the gang decides to go for pizza. You've been told to come straight home and not go anywhere else. Do you:

a. Go with the gang and tell your mom it was a long meeting?

b. Go straight home, since you're not hungry?

c. Call Dad and ask to stay out for the pizza time?

d. Convince the gang to have the pizza delivered so you can stay and eat?

Solution "a" is a decision based on acceptance, not quality.

Solution "b" shows neither acceptance nor quality was important in the decision.

Solution "c" is a decision based on quality.

Solution "d" shows that both quality and acceptance were

185

important in the decision.

It's essential to determine if this situation calls for a quality or acceptance decision or both. If neither are important then a conscientious decision is not required.

Now that you have evaluated your situation and you're considering what's important—quality or acceptance—it's time to ask God for wisdom. Ask and believe that God will give you wisdom. Then get ready for it (James 1:5).

Become a listener. Pay attention to the feeling hidden between the lines (James 1:19).

Help your teen think of alternatives. Write them all down.

Ask the "What would happen" question. "What would happen if you decided to do option 'a' or option 'b,' etc.?" Get your teen to evaluate and describe the possibilities.

Don't make the decision for your teen. If he asks you what you would do, tell him what you'd do and why—only if asked!

If you make a wrong decision, it's not the end of the world. Everyone falls on his face in the dust. That's the way it always has been, and that's the way it always will be.

Coping with Anxiety

Not long back the National Institute of Mental Health announced that the number one mental health problem for adults in America is anxiety. You don't have to have the NIMH do a study to discover that among high schoolers anxiety is considered to be a top-priority mental health problem. We're in great shape, parents and teens worrying all the time. It's too bad there isn't a way to worry away our weight. We would all be skinny.

Parents worry if the kids are dating, and then they worry if they're not. Parents worry when the grades are bad, and then they worry if the grades are all good. Parents even worry when the kid gets a job, and they'll worry when he doesn't have a job. No wonder anxiety is rated number one.

Understanding the Silent Worries

We don't talk much about our worries. Our struggle with anxiety is usually a covert struggle, one that goes on behind the doors of our mind. Most of our fears are imaginary fears— "What if. . . ?" concerns. We don't want others to know we have that kind of fear. So we spend our free hours in front of a TV set or plugged into a stereo, not because we are interested in the pictures or the words. We do it to escape, to hide from our anxieties.

Teens especially seem to be fighting for the worry monkey, and once they get the monkey, they either pretend he's not there or spend all their time playing with him. Consider the following teenagers.

A sixteen-year-old girl, typically shy and plain-looking, worries that she will never get married and that she will be a virgin forever. She dreams daily about meeting the "perfect" young man who loves her for the beauty she has buried beneath her shyness.

An eighteen-year-old senior is anxious about his grades. He needs to have a 3.5 overall grade average to get the scholarship he needs for college. His whole future is in the hands of Mr. Brumbley, his government teacher. He needs an A, and Brumbley only gives a couple of As a year.

A seventeen-year-old, high-strung, easily irritated cheerleader is worried about her boyfriend. He is too possessive and demanding. She is ready to break up with him, but he is the most popular guy at Central High. Nobody has ever broken up with him before. What will her friends think?

I think it is important for teens and parents to understand the anxieties teenagers face. The three examples above are real, and the anxieties are real.

Teens worry about:
grades
friends

romantic relationships
jobs
future
parents

We should encourage teenagers to get in touch with their worries, and then get rid of the monkey. You don't have to have the worry monkey on your back. Give the little critter to God. Put the monkey on His back. The Bible promises, "Humble yourselves, therefore, under God's mighty hand, that he may lift you up in due time. Cast all your anxiety on him because he cares for you" (I Peter 5:6-7).

After a time of prayer with God, set aside some one-on-one-time with your youngster and tell him about a worry that is bugging you. Follow this guideline:

Accept the fear or worry as yours—"Yes, I am worried."
Pray with your teen, giving your worry to God.
Talk to your kid about the worry. Describe it.
Discuss ways that God can help you give up the monkey.
Ask your teen to pray for you.
Expect to be relieved of the worry. Look for peace.

Handling Conflict

Conflict is fascinating. Your task is to infiltrate your teenager's heart and convince him there are better ways to handle conflict than winning, losing or refusing to play the game.

Of course, this can be a frustrating task. Your son or daughter may be really happy with the way he/she handles conflict. Then what do you do?

This task reminds me of a fellow who thought he was dead. He had a close call while in the hospital. During his stay he dreamed that he died and that he was allowed to stay on earth. No one else knew that he died. Once he woke up he was convinced that the dream was real and that he was dead.

His family couldn't convince him otherwise, so they sent him to a psychiatrist. After seven visits, the man still thought he was dead.

At the end of the eighth session the doctor showed the fellow medical books, journals, and diagrams confirming the fact that dead men don't bleed. Finally, the doctor asked, "Do you agree that dead men don't bleed?"

"Yes, I agree."

"Great!" The doctor said as he picked up a needle and pricked the man's finger. Of course, the finger started bleeding, and the doctor asked, "What does that tell you?"

Looking at his bleeding finger, he replied, "My, my! Dead men do bleed!"

You may find that after your best effort, your teen still has not heard what you have been trying to say. Remember, the fence is still up. You are still the parent; you are still responsible for your teen's growth. Firm consequences can help the teen break through to reality and get his act together. Here again, consequences related to the use of the car, the phone, or other family property seem to work best. Working through even the tough times can end up bringing us closer together. What a blessing that is.

Discuss Controversial Issues

Your teen probably knows what you are against, but does he know why? You can be assured that by the time he finishes high school your teen will know someone who has had to deal personally with the problems of drugs, homosexuality, and abortion. It's not enough for parents to use scare tactics about taboo subjects. In fact, that's exactly the wrong thing to do. Instead, when a controversial issue comes up, be willing to sit down and discuss both sides of it.

Teens make smarter decisions when they have factual information and have talked through the issue. Ask your teen to

189

make a list of controversial issues. You make one too. Then plan a family issues night. You might want to invite others in for your discussion evening. Remember, you are not trying to defend what you believe; you are simply talking about topics of concern.

The topics of concern could deal with:
ethics
religion
politics
evolution
war
capital punishment
drugs
sex
death
abortion
pornography

This kind of discussion night will be a great opportunity to practice your listening skills. Please don't turn the time into an evening of anger and argument. The goal is to listen.

Curfew Conflict

One afternoon in chemistry class several teens were comparing notes on how strict and unfair parents are about curfews. In the middle of this negative discussion Barbara stated, "You don't know how lucky you are. I just wish my mother cared enough to set a curfew for me. The best I get is, 'See ya when you get home.' Then when I get home she's always asleep. I think it would be kinda nice to have someone waiting up for me when I get in, someone to hassle me a little, and someone who cared where I was and when I was coming home."

Poor Barbara had a better understanding of her need for limits than her mother did. Conflict about curfews is a covert way of saying, "We love you."

Telling a teen "See ya when you get home" is like telling a four year old, "Stop eating cookies when you've had enough." Although teens need to have their input, it is unrealistic to expect them to set their own curfew limits.

Here are some guidelines to help you set curfews.

10th grade — 11:00 P.M.
11th grade — 11:30 P.M.
12th grade — 12:00 A.M.

If your teen has trouble getting in before the pre-set curfew then determine a consequence that is time related. For example, because he came in one hour late he will have to come in one hour earlier next time.

Critical Attitude

I wonder what would happen if we spent as much time affirming our teens as we do criticizing them? You can be sure of one thing, no matter how bad you think your teens are, there are plenty of parents who would love to trade you problems, if not kids. Expect your teens to be and do their best and they will.

Recently a mother complained that she and her daughter had this heated discussion over what clothes the daughter could wear to church on Wednesday night. "What can I do about it?" she asked.

"I would celebrate. Are you sure that's all you're upset about?" the counselor replied.

"No, she is a great kid. I just think she should dress nicer."

"Listen, I hate to break it to you, but where do you think most of the kids in her high school are on Wednesday nights? Are they in church? And of those who are in church, how many of them want to be there? I want to encourage you to go home and tell your daughter how pleased you are with her desire to attend church, regardless of what she wears."

If your teen is critical all the time, try shocking the conversation with some affirming statements. Keep it up for a week or two, and I guarantee different results. Try:

"I know you put lots of effort into your grades, and I really respect you for working so hard."

"Ever since the day I brought you home from the hospital I've been thankful that you're my daughter."

"You really have a pleasing way about you. I admire the kindness you show others."

"Thanks for being such a cooperative kid. I know some of the hassles you are facing right now, and I think you have really developed great self-control."

"Thanks for being so forgiving of me when I mess up."

Going to Church

Although perfect attendance at church is not a requirement for getting through the Pearly Gates, it can be a problem in some families. Parents have the right to require their teens to go to church as often as the family goes. It is not an option as long as the teens still live at home. That requirement has worked well for lots of kids.

Ron believes flexibility is needed in each situation. We need to find out what's bugging them about church and fix what can be fixed, realizing up front that faith cannot be forced.

Where Is the Monkey?

It has been the goal of *Common Sense Discipline* to help parents and teachers raise resourceful children who will become responsible adults. When this goal is accomplished, the monkey will have been successfully placed on the teenager's back for good and we call him adult.

In order for the goal to be reached, years of patience and faith must be punctuated by letting children make decisions, permitting them to fail, listening to their struggle, helping them succeed, and setting limits where appropriate. At times it is frightening, but it can be one of the greatest adventures of your life. Remember, even after the teens are gone, you can still catch them doing something right!

CHAPTER 11
Coping in the Crisis

11-21 Years

THESE ARE YEARS OF CRISIS. In fact if there does not seem to be a crisis these kids will manufacture one. They live in a tension-filled environment that moves from one crisis to another—the trick is to keep moving. So they fill their lives with activity and distraction.

Crisis Can Bring You Together

Instead of pulling you apart, crisis can push you together. When you face a crisis with your kids, look for the pathway that can bring you together. It's always there, although it's many times well hidden. I pray that you will have eyes to see it. As we examine problem times, keep your eyes open.

Divorce

Divorce is the only form of child abuse sanctioned by society. We now know that young women who may have been able to adjust to the initial crisis of divorce are finding it diffi-cult to make lasting commitments. They are terrified of betrayal.

The last straw is a never-to-be-forgotten image that serves as a flash card to conjure up all the accumulated anger. Divorce's romanticized image as a harmless quick-fix is a lie. Legions have followed this lie into greater unhappiness and pain. Now divorce is not thought of as sin or failure; it's a chance to start over, to celebrate freedom.

One teenage divorce victim stated, "Divorce is a process that never ends. Never! It's not a solution, it's not freedom, it's more like a pain swap shop." Another quipped, "Divorce is like two lions in a den attacking each other. All kids can do is sit behind a window and watch it happen."

One of the most successful ways of helping teens and younger children deal with divorce is found in support groups like Rainbows for All God's Children.

Teenage Depression and Suicide

The following are warning signs of depression:
change in eating habits
feeling helpless
losing interest in doing things
sleeplessness
sudden outbursts of crying
serious drop in grades
extreme fatigue
increased isolation from friends or family
feeling of "Nobody understands"
expressing hostility

Although everyone occasionally feels down or sad, some of us, especially teens, go through periods of depression. If you sense that your teenager is suffering from more than just tem-porary sadness, try getting him or her to:

- Take in an upbeat movie
- Fix something that's broken
- Care for someone's pet
- Exercise
- Learn a new game

It may be that these suggestions don't help. In that case, see a professional counselor immediately. The chances are your teen is thinking about or has considered suicide. Girls attempt suicide ten times more than boys, but boys succeed five times more often than girls. This is serious business. Teens who attempt to kill themselves do it thinking they have lost all other meaningful choices in life. To their way of thinking, death is a choice that no one can take from them. Granted, some teens attempt suicide for attention or to regain control, but the pain's the same.

Communication is the first step toward prevention. Crisis hot lines can provide this first step. Ask your telephone operator for the crisis help or suicide hot line in your area.

If your teenager tells you he has a plan for how to kill himself, call a counselor or the hot line immediately. Never take a threat casually.

Legal Problems

If your teen gets into legal trouble, never, never allow him to spend the night in jail on a first arrest. Consult your attorney as soon as possible and go down and post bond quietly. Avoid a scene in front of the police; save the lectures for later.

If your teen is letting traffic tickets pile up but does nothing about paying them, demand that he pay the tickets or forfeit the use of any car.

Occasionally parents whose teen has been arrested three or four times will ask Roger's advice. After discovering that the parents have paid his bail each time and the teen's behavior has not changed, Roger recommends such parents tell the teen that, since he's a legal adult and certainly knows what the score is, if he gets into trouble with the police again, he will have to accept the consequences for his behavior with no material help from his parents.

That means letting him arrange for his own bail and attorney or take his chances with a court-appointed attorney if he can't afford one. After all, since he's been arrested three times already, he certainly knows what to expect, but he's never had to experience the consequences because someone always bailed him out of trouble.

It is important up front for parents to express their love, but be firm. Bailing him out of trouble only prevents him from learning from the consequences of his actions. Should he be arrested again, assure him that you'll visit him in jail, but that he'll have to arrange how to get out without your help.

Drinking

It's our understanding that the number-one drug problem in America is alcohol abuse. Crack and cocaine get lots of attention, but booze is still number one by far.

If your teen comes home high or drunk, lay out some hard logical consequences for drinking. (Don't try to talk while he is drunk.) For example, you might ground your teen for a weekend; tell him if he comes home high again, he will be grounded for four weekends. As a safety measure, promise him that if he gets high in the future or is with a friend who's driving who can't drive safely, to call you and you'll come get him without making a hassle. The important thing is that your teen still feels like he can call you when he needs help.

Drugs

If you suspect your teen is involved with drugs, get professional help immediately. Ask your physician about local drug abuse programs where parents can get advice and information. If your physician knows of no such programs, contact hospitals, churches, mental health centers, and social service agencies by looking in the phone book. Help is available, so keep asking. Attend meetings and participate in these programs. Get more information about what you can and can't do to help your child. Ask questions, get sound advice, and then follow it.

Often, the people who can best help drug abusers are recovered abusers themselves, much the same way members of Alcoholics Anonymous help each other.

Never kick a child out of the house when you suspect a drug abuse or an emotional problem. When kids get into the habit of abusing privileges or taking advantage of their parents' good will, some action needs to be taken, but not all at once and not without serious consideration to possible consequences. The problems that run beneath drug abuse go much deeper than the surface, and counseling by experienced professionals is always needed.

When a Teenager Refuses

Occasionally a teenager will become totally uncooperative and disobedient. It's as though he is testing you to see if you're still willing to lead. If you're not, he'll take over. In one case, where drugs were not an issue, parents of a rebellious son consulted a therapist. This was their decision: One day while their son was at school, both parents went to his room and stripped it completely. He was left with his bed, dresser and the clothes in his closet. Gone were his posters, stereo and records, and other assorted junk. When he came home that afternoon he stared at his room in disgust and then turned angrily to his parents and demanded, "Where's my stuff?"

They replied something like this: "We put your things in storage. If you want your things back, you will have to earn them back, one at a time, by acting more courteous with us and cooperating around the house. If you don't want to cooperate with us, your things will remain in storage."

In just a few short days the teen became more responsible and polite. Gradually he earned back his things by negotiating with his parents, finding out what was expected of him, and then acting better around the house. Now, a number of years later, he's grown and a fine young man. Most parents would consider him a source of pride now. But for a while the situation looked desperate. Parents need to remember: Desperate situations call for desperate action.

Gangs

The most effective way to get a teen disengaged from a gang is to first discover the reason(s) for the youth's involvement, then match that engagement reason with one of the following disengagement reasons:

1. Teens lose interest as they get older.

2. Teens realize the gang's promises were an illusion.

3. Teens become frightened by the gang's activities.

4. Teens become terrified by some threat to the gang.

5. Teens realize that they are being controlled by gang leaders.

6. Teens realize they aren't so unpredictable, that they fit a typical profile of gang members. To those that know gangs, their actions are not surprising.

7. Family problems are addressed and relationships are restored.

8. Teens find someone who can help them deal with their pain.

Sex for the Wrong Reasons

Teenagers get involved sexually for a lot of reasons. Many times the bottom line is not love. The following list has been compiled from interviews with teens who are active sexually.

1. Affection—Seeking sexual intimacy out of a desire for closeness.

2. Animosity—Venting hostility toward parents by having sex with someone.

3. Anxiety—Using sex as a temporary relief from frustrations.

4. Boredom—Seeking sex as a momentary break from a boring routine.

5. Mending wounds—Using sex as a way to make up after an argument or to forget one's troubles.

6. Accomplishments—Keeping up with peers or "scoring," because it seems to be what is expected.

7. Recreation—Engaging in sex for the fun of it.

8. Lust—Engaging in sex to relieve sexual hunger.

If Your Daughter Is Pregnant

If your teenage daughter tells you she thinks she's pregnant, before you try to decide on a plan of action, pray together for God to help both of you deal with the emotions of the moment. First, have her examined by a physician. Then consider these options for you and your daughter:

1. Remain single and allow the baby to be adopted.

2. Remain single and allow the baby to be raised by other relatives.

3. Remain single and keep the baby.

4. Marry and keep the baby.

Adoption

Placing the baby for adoption can be accomplished by your daughter finishing her pregnancy at home and attending her own school or completing the school year with home teachers until delivery. Or you can arrange for your daughter to live away from home until after the birth by: 1) Staying in a home for unwed mothers, 2) Staying in an approved foster home, or 3) Staying in informal foster care with a relative or trusted friend.

To learn more about any of these options, talk with a social worker. You can ask your physician, minister, or a social ser-vice agency. Usually there is no charge for this consultation, and it will ease your worries to talk things over with someone who has helped others with this problem.

Keeping the Baby

Some parents may want to help their daughter raise her baby at home or place it with other relatives out of a sense of obligation. Usually this is discouraged. To encourage a teenager to keep an unexpected, out-of-wedlock baby is approving of children being raised by children. It's one thing for teenage girls to baby-sit, but raising a child on a full-time basis is something altogether different.

Marriage

The subsequent divorce rate for teenagers who married because they were pregnant is about ninety percent. Due to the problems, such as resentment and almost certain divorce, we wouldn't even give this option serious thought. Our advice is this: Parents, if you really love that baby, arrange for adoption through a legitimate child-care agency; then wait for grandkids who are planned and wanted.

Dropping Out of School

Sometimes teenagers do so poorly in school and fail so much that, in frustration, they decide to drop out. There are few things that cause parents more anguish. If your teenager is threatening to drop out of school, definitely seek professional counseling. Both of you could probably benefit from several sessions together. Even if he won't go, you go. It will be money well spent.

The prodigal son (Luke 15) was such a case. Apparently he had all the benefits of a good family, but one day he decided to leave it all. The Scriptures give no record of anything his father might have said to stop him from going, though we can imagine what many parents would be tempted to say: "Don't you think this is premature? Are you sure you want to do this? Look, let's talk about it. I think you're getting ready to make the biggest mistake of your life." But no such arguments are recorded. Instead, the prodigal's father, recognizing there was little he could do or say to keep his son from leaving, decided to split the inheritance between his two sons. The youngest went on his way without hearing so much as, "You're going to be sorry."

After the boy had made the inevitable mess of his life, he returned home begging forgiveness and seeking only shelter and a job as a hired hand. Fortunately for him, his father's unconditional love and forgiveness were complete; his family relationship and his future were restored.

Like this father, parents have times when there aren't good decisions to make, only painful ones, from which they must pick the best of the bad choices at hand. Like the decision of a surgeon faced with amputation of an infected limb or doing nothing and allowing an infection to spread, sometimes parents have to pick the lesser of the two unpleasant choices. That's what the prodigal's father did.

Notice that the father didn't throw his son's failure up to him or say, "I told you so." Remaining silent is a painful decision to make, especially when we think our kids are about to make the mistake of their lives. But sometimes being silent is the best thing to do. Occasionally rebellion has to take its course before repentance can come about.

Looking Back

We've talked about lots of different problems in this chapter. Hopefully, your family will never need this information, but occasionally circumstances are beyond our control. No family is immune to problems. Parents who attend church regularly sometimes seem shocked when they discover a major problem in their family and are often reluctant to seek help until things can wait no longer. Often we hear parents say, "I feel like if I were just a better Christian or prayed more then I wouldn't be having these problems." Being a good Christian doesn't immunize one against broken bones or heart attacks; neither does it lessen the chance of emotional and behavioral problems. We wish it did, but it doesn't.

Problems do, however, give us a chance to see our weaknesses and discover God's strengths. And the bad times can bring us closer together. Never stop praying for eyes to see the pathway of reconciliation. God can melt even the most stubborn heart. He is in the business of turning hearts of children to their parents and the hearts of parents to their young (Malachi 4:5-6).

CHAPTER 12
Challenges to Your Plans

Single Parenthood

ONE IN FOUR CHILDREN IS NOW living in a single parent family. In most of these situations, the single parent is a mother who will experience following stresses:

loss of identity

overwhelming feelings of being left out and alone

changing rules, growing frustrations, and ever-present fear of doing/saying the wrong thing

guilt and shame and the prevailing sense of being "one sandwich shy of a picnic"

aimlessness and feeling disconnected—lost in the wilderness

bitterness and resentment

bouncing from one crisis to another

feeling tired and drained

money worries

custody concerns

Single parent families need the "extended-family" that is present in churches. Here's what your church could do to help:

• Give hugs every now and then.

• Include single parents in social gatherings of families, for example, holiday get-togethers.

• Develop a skill bank, a co-op for parents who can help each other.

• Provide training and support programs for single parents.

• Consider developing a church fund for helping single parent families through difficult times.

• Speak out as an advocate of single parents and their unique situations.

• Give single parents significant tasks in your church. Don't overwork them, but give them the opportunities that will help close the door on the past.

Differences in Kids

The waitress had just poured our second cup of coffee when Gary explained, "As I see it there are four things that are certain: God is still in charge. Dead people don't bleed. I'll never make enough money. No two kids are put together the same."

Judy responded, "I'm glad our kids are different. It would be boring to be just like someone else. Every morning would begin with, 'Are you real or are you Memorex.'"

Judy has the right attitude about differences. It's our differences that make us special. Each youngster has distinctive differences in birth order, experiences, problems, energy, agenda, boundary requirements, and abilities. The sooner you are able to recognize and accept your youngster's differences, the sooner you will be able to help him use his differences as building blocks for confidence.

Birth Order Personality

Being first, second or third in the family lineup tends to

affect a child's personality regardless of what the parents do. If you're wondering which place is best, the truth is that there's good news and bad news for any position. As parents prepare themselves to raise thinking, responsible children, the first step is understanding that each child will be different. That's OK; in fact, it's good! The following descriptions of typical children are intended to point out the naturalness of differences. As you read, reflect on and evaluate your own situation.

Oldest Children

As a group, firstborn children tend to walk, talk and do most of the "baby book" things earlier than other children. As the only child in the family, firstborns mostly have adults to copy, and so they strive to mimic grown-up actions early. Because there isn't an older brother or sister around to help them, elders have to learn to do things for themselves.

First-time parents tend to be more cautious about the way they raise their first child. The oldest becomes a guinea pig in a new parenting system and so usually gets an overdose of protection. Consequently, firstborn kids tend to be more cautious and conservative than their younger brothers and sisters. They tend to be higher achievers, more serious-minded, less sociable. They generally make better grades and cause fewer problems in school. At times they seem to be model kids. Better watch out, though, because the pressure to be models— "But you're the oldest, and you know better! I can't believe you would do that!"—is hard for some kids to handle. One disadvantage of being an oldest child is he generally has a "work" attitude about play and entertainment. Firstborns tend to be compulsive about tasks and may have trouble relaxing or just doing nothing. They may accept the values and beliefs of parents without really questioning the concepts and making them their own.

Firstborn Girls

Even in homes where both parents work outside the home, the firstborn girl always gets an abundance of attention from Mom. While small, the firstborn is around Mom almost without interruption and tries hard to be like Mom. Soon she becomes Mother's little helper, and the pleasant remarks that Mom and Dad make about her helpful nature encourage her to act that way. It's no accident that most nurses and schoolteachers are oldest or only daughters. From their early years on, they copy the actions they see Mother do.

When brothers and sisters come along, some normal childhood jealousy is probably inevitable, but older girls soon discover that the surest way to lose favor with Mom and Dad is to be mean to the baby. At one time she had all of their attention, but now she has to share it with the baby. She discovers the way to get back into her parents' favor is to help out. Soon she learns to get diapers and brings them to Mom, tries to make the baby happy by bringing a toy and often tries to help with the bottle. Naturally, Mom appreciates all of this new source of help and continues to praise her little helper with remarks like, "You're a good big sister. You're Mother's best helper." It's easy to see why she grows up as a "helper" and "caretaker." Parents will frequently leave a small child in the care of an older sister at an age when they wouldn't think of allowing someone else in the neighborhood to baby-sit.

Firstborn Boys

The firstborn son, whether he is the first or second child, tends to be more responsible and a higher achiever than later kids. After other children are born, he becomes the big brother and readily assumes that role, acting protective and sometimes bossy. Older boys tend to act more responsibly.

How many times have you heard well-meaning friends and relatives say to the older of two children, "You'd better watch out or your little brother will catch up with you." While this remark is usually said in jest when comparing height or some such thing, the oldest is likely to take it literally and become worried about being passed up. To the youngest, a comment like that is music to his ears because nothing would suit him better than to be bigger. But the oldest doesn't want to lose his position, and so he works that much harder at excelling and achieving.

Even some of the family conflicts described in the Bible involve an older brother who felt outdone by a younger. Such was the case with Cain and Abel and with Esau and Jacob.

Middlers Are Moderates

Just as being the first child in a family leaves its imprint, so does being the middle child. Middle children generally are less academically oriented than oldest children, but tend to be more socially adept. They grow up playing with three sets of friends—their own, their older brother's or sister's, and their younger brother's or sister's. Middle children learn what works best with older and younger children and so get along well with all kinds of people. Because the oldest child had already carved out a niche in the family's history by being the first to walk, talk, go to school, and ride a bike, the middle child accepts that there are few firsts for him. Consequently, he may go off on an entirely different tangent in his personality, if only to show his parents and others that "I'm different."

This difference is especially pronounced in elementary school where there have been several other children from the same family who did well. By the time Junior comes along he's heard for the hundredth time, "Oh, so you're so and so's little brother/sister. We certainly enjoyed having your brother and sister." Better watch that line because it may be a set up for a "big" surprise. You see, that younger child has had to follow in big brother/sister's footsteps for so long that he's just dying to strike out on his own. When you tell him what you most admired about his older brother (grades, cooperation, attitudes, etc.), he's likely to do just the opposite to express his own individuality, if only to say, "I may have the same last name, but that's all we have in common." Remember, everyone is different.

The Baby Syndrome

Being the "baby" is tough. You gets lots of attention for being the youngest, and, of course, that feels good. But there is always an older brother or sister nearby who is impatient and wants you to hurry up. You can't help it if you're slow; you're just not grown-up yet. Older kids get impatient and rescue the youngest, saying, "Here, let me do it for you." After a time you decide to let them do your work because, "If you can't beat 'em, might as well join 'em." Since you have so many "parents" around telling you what to do, you sometimes tend to be more docile and passive.

Youngest children tend to be more laid back and less achievement-oriented than their older brothers and sisters. At the same time, they also learn to manipulate those around them, like Jacob did Esau: "If they're going to treat me like a baby, at least I'm going to make it work for me on my terms." The baby of the family may find it most helpful to act helpless. It may be in the high school years before the youngest begins to assert herself/himself.

Parents can foster this dependent attitude by developing a habit of rescuing their youngest. Children are frequently brought to Roger's office with one problem or another, usually school related. When Roger asks the child a question, there is often a pause while the child looks at Mom. She dutifully answers for him. After two or three pauses of that sort, Roger will look directly at the child and say, "Usually when I have a child who always looks to Mom before answering, or who pauses before answering, I know I have a situation where the youngest has trained Mom to answer for him. He knows if he waits long enough, Mom will always answer for him. That's already happened three times today. Is that what you're doing? Are you stalling on purpose because you know Mom will come to your rescue and answer for you?"

Both Mom and the kid suddenly see what's been happening. Even then the kid will look to Mom for her response, though by this time she's determined to remain quiet. Finally, the child agrees that the training program really works.

Age-Spread Difference

Usually when four or more years separate one child from the next in line, the younger will often act like the oldest of a second set of children. Because of their spread in ages they are too far apart to be close and compete with each other's accomplishments.

Parents may say, "But we raised them just alike"; however, that's not humanly possible. Your lifestyle has changed, and you most certainly have mellowed with age. Though two children's heredity may be almost identical, their environment is different. With each succeeding child, parents usually have more disposable income, they're older, more experienced and, therefore, more relaxed about child rearing. You may recall hearing or saying, "But you never let me do that when I was that age!"

Emotional Stress
Experiences with Death

A child who has experienced the death of a sibling learns a lot about life. Whatever the reason for a child's death—accident, illness or birth defect—the child closest in age may feel responsible. That's due in most part to the surviving child's normal degree of rivalry, competition, and resentment. When a child dies, what had been resentment develops into guilt that the surviving child's feelings contributed to the death.

The next child born after the death of an older child will

likely be handled with kid gloves, sheltered and overly pro-
tected. Such a child is much more likely to act immaturely for
his age, even more so than the usual "baby" phenomenon.

Moving

Moving can be a total disaster or it can be a blessing in dis-
guise. The current trend shows the average child moves six
times before graduating from high school. A move, especially
to a different city or state can have positive or negative effects
on children's personalities. Changes and promotions in parents' jobs can cause changes in responsibilities and responses,
and pressures on parents. When parents change their lifestyle,
their change naturally modifies the child's lifestyle too.

Moving represents a time of starting over and developing
new aspects of identity and personality. Some therapists actually support moving as a healthy way to handle difficult problems.

Handicaps

At times handicapped children will feel like they have a
giant neon sign on their heads. The sign is continually flashing "defective, defective, defective." Simply having the handicap tends to result in his receiving "special" parental treatment. Usually this is through overindulgence, excessive
sympathy or an overly protective manner.

One of the most fascinating jobs Roger has held involved
rehabilitation work with visually-impaired children and
adults. For three years he talked with interesting people with
a variety of visual problems ranging from loss of one eye to
complete blindness. Over and over Roger was impressed by a
consistent attitude among adults who were blind. Conversation went something like this:

"Roger, you sighted people often do us blind folks a disser-
vice by the way you treat us."

Roger recalls,

In the middle of trying to help, I felt a little

defensive when I heard those words. I really felt we had all been extremely thoughtful. "How's that?" I asked.

"You often feel sorry for us and try to make things easier for us. I'll tell you something, Roger. Since they can't transplant eyes yet, the sooner a blind kid learns to walk with a cane by himself and to read Braille, the sooner he's going to accept his handicap and become independent. That's tough, but that's the way it is."

Over the years since then, it's been Roger's experience that whenever a child's handicap can't be corrected through surgery or therapy, the sooner that child's parents help him adjust and cope with the handicap, the better off the child will be. Parents, if your child has any sort of handicap, don't intensify the problem by indulging him. The sooner he learns to live and cope with it, the better for all concerned.

Temperamental Differences

Some kids have a stem that seems always to be wound too tight. They are just born that way. Some babies are easy, while some are average in temperament. A few are difficult and seem especially fussy; they may be prone to colic or catch every possible childhood disease and illness, and may even be ultrasensitive to any change in their environment. Fortunately, these kinds of biological problems may disappear by the time the child reaches puberty.

What Is Hyperactivity?

What about the child who may be hyperactive? One of the primary reasons Roger gets referrals from pediatricians is suspected hyperactivity. Hyperactivity is an overused term. I have heard it used to describe anything from acting restless to neurological impairment. It's been my experience that the vast majority of children referred to me as hyperactive are, in fact, emotionally nervous but not biologically hyperactive. Understanding the difference is important because biological hyperactivity may require medical treatment, while psychological hyperactivity can usually be handled by using common sense discipline techniques. There are two questions to ask yourself when you suspect a child is hyperactive:

1. "Can this child watch TV for at least thirty minutes, if it's a program he/she enjoys, without getting up or getting restless, except during commercials?"

2. "Is this hyperactivity present only with certain people in certain settings?"

If your answer to both questions is "No," then the child is probably biologically hyperactive. But if either question is answered "Yes," the problem is likely not biological.

Over and over I've heard parents respond to the TV question with, "Oh, if it's something he likes to watch, like Saturday morning cartoons, he can sit for two hours straight, almost without moving a muscle." In my opinion, there's little chance such a kid is biologically hyperactive. That's important, because too many parents and some physicians are too quick to put these kids on medication to control their hyperactivity.

Don't Jump to Conclusions

I've heard teachers label a child hyperactive, while other teachers describe him as typical. In such cases somebody has misdiagnosed the problem. Perhaps the teacher is the one who needs medication.

As for those rare occasions when you answer no to both questions suggesting true biological hyperactivity, first check with his teachers for verification. It may be that there is only a clash of personalities between you and the child. If his teachers all report that he is hyper with them, and most of

214

them have been using common sense discipline techniques with him for at least two weeks with poor results, refer the student to the school counselor. If that doesn't help, and if the counselor concurs that the student appears hyperactive, consider having him evaluated by a qualified psychologist. Yes, he may still not be genuinely hyperactive.

For the sake of your child, have him evaluated by someone who knows how to change misbehavior with common sense methods. Remember, the majority of children referred to Roger with suspected hyperactivity were only emotionally nervous and responded well to common sense discipline without needing to be medicated for their hyperactivity.

Should Hyper Kids Be Medicated?

A problem occurs when a child has been placed on medication for hyperactivity and it "works." Parents may erroneously conclude that their child was genuinely biologically hyperactive. That may not be the case, for the child may simply be drugged to the point that all anxiety and excessive movement are held in check by the medication.

When a child is hyper for psychological reasons, he/she is generally waving an emotional red flag that says, "Hey, look at me. I need more attention. I need help." Sometimes the hyperactivity disappears simply with additional parental attention. Someone has said that the best thing parents can give their children is time. To children, time is attention.

Hyper with a Message

Sometimes hyperactivity goes away with a bit more structure or guidelines at home. For example, some children act up because they don't know what's expected of them. This kind of hyperactivity is not physical or emotional; it's learned behavior. It's as if they have adopted the attitude, "If I just keep on testing Mom and Dad, sooner or later they'll lay down the law to me." Unfortunately, too many parents don't.

Consistency Calms Kids

Children are most calm when they know what's expected of them and what things they can do that will automatically gain parental approval. On the other hand, if they don't know what to do to get approval, or they don't know when to expect punishment, then they tend to go "crazy" and test the water. Here's where consistency fits in. It's easier for a child to deal with two parents who can't seem to get it together between them, than to deal with one parent who has different standards from one moment to the next. Parents and teachers should be as consistent and as predictable as possible.

Putting Differences to Use

OK, so they're different because of a number of things including birth order and biology. How can we capitalize on the differences? Proverbs 22:6 puts it this way, "Train up a child in the way he should go, and when he is old he will not turn from it." The point is that every child has a unique "way" to go. Each child is an original with a personal destiny.

If parents will look for the differences and develop the best of the differences, then they will be preparing their child for a life-long adventure with life.

First, recognize and appreciate those differences by encouraging your children to develop their individual talents. One may be better academically while another may have better musical or artistic skills. Instead of comparing them by saying, "Why aren't you good at math like your sister?" you can compliment their differences by saying, "You are each good in different areas, and that's fine with me. In school I hope you'll do as well as you can in all of your subjects."

Second, encourage your children to value each other's accomplishments. Our next-door neighbors have four children. The three boys all did well in sports, and their younger sister went with Mom and Dad to watch them play. When her piano recitals came around, Mom and Dad told her brothers they were expected to go. Like normal brothers they said, "Mom, do we have to go?"

"Yes, she went with us to watch you play, and now it's your turn to watch her play."

Third, be glad your children are different. It shows you're allowing them to grow up individually, not like cookies cut from the same mold. The more their individuality is recognized the less reason they'll have to rebel later.

Different Kids, Same Needs

One of the most vivid descriptions of favoritism in the Bible is found in the Genesis 37 story of Joseph and his eleven brothers. Born when Jacob was an old man, Joseph was the next-to-youngest son. He was his father's favorite and was singled out for special attention by Jacob's gift of a fancy, one-of-a-kind robe. Jacob's favoritism proved to be Joseph's undoing. His brothers began resenting him for the special attention, and finally they arranged to get rid of him by selling Joseph into slavery.

After years of Egyptian bondage, Joseph rose in rank in the Egyptian court until he became the second highest administrator in the land (Genesis 41:40). When famine hit Canaan, Jacob sent his sons to Egypt to buy grain. Unknown to them at first, their once-hated brother became their source of hope. God took what they did out of resentment and turned it into something He meant for good.

This story has an important message for parents—don't play favorites, especially when there are stepchildren or half-brothers and half-sisters involved. While it's natural to feel special toward one's youngest child, the older children still have their need for attention, especially as they go through the difficult teenage years. If you have stepchildren, don't try to take the place of their other parent. You will never be the natural parent. It's normal to feel more love, at least at first, for your biological children. Still, you can make the effort to give each child individualized time and attention.

A father came to see me because of the trouble he was having getting along with his teenage stepson. The boy moved with his mother and sister into the house the man had owned for a number of years. Right away the stepson felt out of place, especially since his stepfather had two older sons who were already well-established in the neighborhood.

"What can I do to make him like me?" the father asked me. "Right now, he can't stand me."

I talked to the father and learned that his job required him to go to different locations, calling on customers and seeing if equipment repairs or adjustments were needed.

"When your own kids were younger," I asked him, "did you ever take them with you on service calls?"

"Sure, all the time on weekends and when school was out."

"Okay, here's what you do. Next time you have a service call to make, ask him if he'd like to go along."

"What if he says he doesn't want to go or thinks I'm trying to butter him up?"

"Oh, he probably will at first, so expect it; but say something like you thought he might be interested in going along to see what you do or just for the ride."

As expected, the stepson balked at first. "Why me? Do I have to?"

"No, just thought you might like to." Then the stepfather wisely added, "Bill and Jack enjoyed going with me when they were your age, and I thought you might have fun coming along too."

At first the stepson avoided going, and his stepfather was discouraged at being rebuffed. I encouraged him to keep asking because the message was bound to get through eventually. Sure enough, on the third invitation, the boy jumped at the chance, and a healthy relationship was born.

In a newly blended stepfamily, it's normal for stepchildren to feel out of place. They may act edgy and on the defensive as they feel their way around. Be patient with them, offer them support and love, but don't expect them to accept you at first. They're only testing you. Stay with it, and you'll probably be rewarded by their acceptance.

When you get serious about raising responsible children, it's important to invest time in understanding each child's differences. The birth-order differences, unique life experiences, special problems and various energy levels can become strengths. If we can view these differences as strengths instead of weaknesses or defects we will be influential in helping our children take advantage of their differences. And, helping our children in this task is what common sense discipline is about.

POSTSCRIPT:
Resources for Staying in Balance

RULES ARE LIKE WINTER CLOTHING. If you put them on all at once, especially before it's necessary, you can smother. Just as it's easy to make a young child frustrated from too many layers of unnecessary clothing, it's easy to lay on too many rules that aren't necessary. Few parents or teachers will need all of these rules. Some definitely will not apply to your children, so use your judgment.

Making Rules That Work

To be effective rules must be:

Simple—Kids must be able to repeat them and understand them.

Firm—Rules are not bent by a flimsy excuse.

Fair—They are applied equally to all children.

Flexible—They can be adjusted to fit the circumstances.

Rules are like fences. They need to be firm and strong to do the job for which they're intended, but they also need to be flexible in case something unexpected happens. Don't forget some kids require more rules than others; that's just the way kids are.

Homework Rules

1. After school, no TV until homework's done.

2. I won't do homework for you, but I'll help.

3. If you miss an assignment, you can call a friend or your teacher to get the assignment.

4. If you fall behind, you will have to study on weekends.

5. I expect you to earn your grades without cheating.

6. No telephone calls while you are studying, unless it's about the assignment.

7. If you need me to drive you to the library for extra resources, I'll be glad to if you give me enough advance notice.

8. You are responsible for remembering your assignments and keeping up with your materials and books.

Rules for Meals

1. Come to breakfast after you have dressed and taken care of your room.

2. Be polite about seconds. Ask if others would like something else first.

3. You may have dessert after you have eaten an appropriate portion of your meal.

4. When we finish our meals we all rinse our plates and put them in the sink/dishwasher.

5. After a meal, everyone helps by clearing the table and putting away leftover food.

6. Clean up after yourself when you make a snack.

7. You are responsible for serving your friends snacks while they are here and for cleaning up any mess they might make.

8. You are expected to share in the chores of cooking, cleaning up and putting away groceries.

9. We eat only in the kitchen or dining rooms.

Rules about Pets

1. You are responsible for feeding your pet.

2. Your pet needs regular attention and play times.

3. You will be expected to bathe your pet and clean its house/cage/litterbox when I tell you it's time.

4. If you fail to take care of your pet, then I may sell it or give it to another child who will provide better care for it.

Rules about Gifts

1. You should always write a thank-you note.

2. I will be happy to help you word a thank-you note if you first get the paper and pencils.

Rules about Phone Calls

1. On school nights, if your homework is finished, you may use the phone until 9:00 P.M.

2. There are to be no phone calls after 9:00 P.M. If someone calls you after that time, I'll take a message.

3. If you tie up the phone for more than fifteen minutes at a time, you may lose your phone privileges for the next day.

Bedtime Rules for Preschoolers

1. I will tuck you in bed once and read a story.

2. If you can't sleep, you may look at books or play quietly so long as you stay in bed and you don't disturb the rest of us.

3. After you brush your teeth for the night, no more snacks.

4. Once you go to bed, you are welcome to get all the water you want, but you will have to get it yourself.

Rules for TV

1. No TV in the mornings on school days. On weekends, no TV until you've had breakfast and picked up your room.

2. No TV in the evenings until you've completed all your homework.

3. If the TV is too loud, I'll ask you once to turn it down. If the sound remains too loud, you will have to turn the TV off for thirty minutes.

4. You may watch only those shows we agree on ahead of time and that we've circled together in the TV schedule.

Classroom Rules

1. Because we recognize our collective responsibility to this class we will arrive on time, in an orderly fashion, ready to participate and study.

2. We will behave in a polite and considerate manner that permits each one to study and learn.

3. We will respect each person's right to dignity. Negative remarks about one's family, birthplace, race, or religion will be considered insults and will be considered inappropriate at school.

4. We will respect each other's property. We consider the school building(s), equipment and grounds our collective property.

5. We will earn our grades fairly and honestly with dignity. We will not brag or ridicule about grades.

6. Exceptional behavior in this class will be recognized appropriately. Students with excellent grades and those with exceptional improvement will be acknowledged. Students whose actions detract from the learning environment can expect to receive consequences in front of the class.

7. We will accept our responsibility to encourage and correct each other when necessary.

8. We will apologize when appropriate.

9. We recognize that violations of these rules will be subject to consequences set by our school's district administrators, teachers and our class's student disciplinary committee. (Note: This may be an ad hoc committee.)